ZERO LEADS

The Secret To Growing A 7-Figure Freelance Business... Without Any Leads

JAMES BRAY

ZERO LEADS
The Secret To Growing A 7-Figure Freelance Business…Without Any Leads

Copyright @ 2021. James Bray. All rights reserved. No part of this book may be reproduced by any mechanical, photographic, or electronic process, or in the form of a phonographic recording; nor may it be stored in a retrieval system, transmitted, or otherwise be copied for public or private use—other than for "fair use" as brief quotations embodied in articles and reviews—without prior written permission of the publisher.

This publication is designed to provide accurate and authoritative information regarding the subject matter covered. It is sold with the understanding that the publisher is not engaged in rendering legal, accounting, or other professional services. If you require legal advice or other expert assistance, you should seek the services of a competent professional.

Design and cover art by James Bray.

Disclaimer: The author makes no guarantees to the results you'll achieve by reading this book. All business requires risk and hard work. The results and client case studies presented in this book represent results achieved working directly with the author. Your results may vary when undertaking any new business venture or marketing strategy.

To my amazing wife Alanah and my two awesome children, Livia and Elsie, who've supported me through the good times and the bad, and who've helped me find my freedom.

FOREWORD

If I had to describe James Bray in 3 words, it'd be "business with soul".

On paper, Zero Leads is everything I'm against. James doesn't like sales funnels. He doesn't like building massive email lists. He doesn't like webinar sales!? Seriously?!

And then as I read Zero Leads, it became more and more apparent that I agreed with him. The tools that are sold by online marketing gurus and hype-preneurs such as sales funnels and cookie-cutter webinars are absolutely awful. And the biggest lie sold to freelance business owners? That you need more leads.

James and I met when we were consulting at a telco company. I told him a little about what I did, and I remember us connecting immediately over "new-marketing". Both of us were frustrated at the corporate model and the way traditional sales and marketing operated. We'd both experienced larger corporate marketing and we knew that there were some fundamental flaws in what they were doing. The spend on ads, events, sponsorship and all the other huge expenses seemed crazy to us. Why do all that, when you could easily create a podcast with a following and sell to people with relationships based on content?

When I first started Sell Your Service, I wish I had this book. I was running Sell Your Service when I first met James and I had all the things he talks about in this book. Sales funnels, automations, webinars, sales pages and...it wasn't working. Years later, I was looking at my balance sheet and scratching my head again thinking "what was I missing?" Revenue was down, but our leads were at an all-time high?

This is why this book is so important. And also, why I said James Bray is business with soul. You see, what James understands more than most, is that all the tools and platforms and methods mean NOTHING without a little of you in the mix. In fact, all the webinars and sales pages in the world won't mean jack unless you've got you AND the customer in the mix. You need a little madness in the method.

My problem was that I was running campaigns and expecting the process to do the heavy lifting. But I wasn't putting enough of me and my story AND I wasn't telling enough of the customer story in my content. I'm from an old-school sales background and my method of selling was (is? lol) keep selling until they buy.

One of the things that would drive James bananas, was the corporate messaging, adverts and collateral put out, on a budget of tens of thousands, but it had zero soul. It had no personality, no relationship. It talked about the business, not the people. It talked about the features, not the customer or their story. James was insistent on getting more customer stories even then, because as he put it "the customer writes the copy if you'll let them".

In this book, you'll see some hyper-pragmatic and specific tools you can use to put your soul and the customer story into your sales and marketing. I wish I'd had this when I was starting. This is coupled with my lead generation/revenue problem. What wasn't working? I finally realised after reading through this book a few times, that my problem was my maths and focus were all wrong. I was so obsessed with generating leads, that I had neglected my sales approach. Pretty poor show from a company CALLED Sell Your Service. Revenue and profit are found as soon as you land the customer. It's up to you to find it. So, take it from me, as someone who generates thousands of leads a month, that lead generation means NOTHING unless you implement a Zero Leads method in your business.

James is business with soul. I've never met anyone who gets this stuff so easily AND who gets so excited to share it with others. I'm extremely proud to call James my friend and I know you're going to love this book.

Have courage, commit and take action.

Mike Killen
Founder, Sell Your Service

CONTENTS

INTRODUCTION — 1
TODAY IS A GREAT DAY — 2
TWO SIMPLE REASONS — 4

PERSPECTIVE SHIFT — 9
EARN MORE, BE MORE — 10
WHO THIS BOOK (AND METHOD) IS FOR — 14
THE 5 BARRIERS TO PROFITABLE GROWTH — 19
WHY YOU DON'T NEED (OR WANT) LEADS IN YOUR BUSINESS — 45
THE #1 PROBLEM WITH A ZERO LEADS APPROACH — 54

THE ZERO LEADS FRAMEWORK — 59
THE MARBLE RUN — 60
HOW TO CONSISTENTLY ATTRACT 5-FIGURE CLIENTS…FOR FREE — 80
HOW TO GO FROM "JUST MET" TO $50,000 PROJECT — 102

CREATING YOUR SIGNATURE OFFER — 120
HOW TO DEFINE YOUR UNIQUE FRAMEWORK — 121
THE FIVE FIGURE DROP — 131
HOW TO COME UP WITH IRRESISTIBLE PRODUCT IDEAS — 142

THE BUSINESS OF BELIEF — 151
HOW TO MAXIMISE CONVERSIONS (AND PROFIT) — 152
BUILDING YOUR ZERO LEADS TEAM — 160
GETTING STARTED WITH YOUR PRODUCTS — 164
GETTING STARTED ON YOUR BELIEF MACHINE — 172

REALISING YOUR POTENTIAL — 179
WHAT TO DO NEXT? — 180
HOW TO GET MORE HELP — 183
ABOUT THE AUTHOR — 186

INTRODUCTION

TODAY IS A GREAT DAY

Today is the best day we have.

In fact, today is the only day we have. Yesterday has finished. Tomorrow is yet to come.

Today is the only day we have to make the changes we want to see in our lives, happen.

Today you've started reading this book. Today you've made a conscious decision to change. And you're acting upon it. That puts you in a place above 99% of the rest of the world's population.

Only the brave choose to change. Only the determined do something about it.

There's no better time in history for anyone to be able to radically transform their lives, than today. Today, opportunities to better our lives and the lives of others around us are everywhere. The barriers to entry have disappeared. What once was the luxury of a select few is now open to all…if we choose to grasp it.

Today you can learn. Today you can improve. Today you can get closer to the life you desire.

Today I want to thank you. For deciding to give me your precious time and attention by reading this book. I promise I will not waste it.

Today is the start of something special.

Today is a great day…

TWO SIMPLE REASONS

"Stories cannot be owned. Stories should not be owned. Stories are the shared experiences between ourselves and the many. What may be our story becomes their story when told. When we tell our story we let others in. We engage, we teach, we understand. We bond. Stories resonate when we see ourselves in them. When we feel ourselves in them. To tell your story is to tell the stories of a million others. Those that share your passions, your values, your beliefs. When you next tell your story, remember, it's their story you're telling."

--

There are three (very closely related) values that I hold above everything else:

Honesty, respect and no bullshit.

Therefore, I'm going to open this book staying true to those values.

I wrote this book for two simple reasons:

- **Reason #1:** A sales tool. In the hope that once you've read through it, you'll hire me and my team to help you implement the **Zero Leads** system in your own business.

- **Reason #2:** A results tool. To help you start getting positive results in your business immediately, so you'll want to do Reason #1 ASAP.

Throughout this book, I'm not going to preach to you. I'm not going to disrespect you with false claims and a rose-tinted perspective. I'm not going to use it as a thinly veiled sales pitch. I don't need (or want) to do that.

Instead of all that tiresome nonsense that so many "experts" use to take your money, I'm simply going to help you.

I'm going to help you start seeing a change for the better in your business through the method I use day-in, day-out to grow my business.

And if I help you enough in these pages, you can then decide if you'd like to talk to us further about working together.

This book is a combination of my methodology and philosophy in growing a successful and profitable service business. In the first few chapters, we'll be looking at the current myths and misconceptions around "lead-generation". A lot of "experts" have been teaching a standard method of getting new leads that I believe is not only **outdated**, but fundamentally **wrong**.

We'll look at the reasons behind this and more importantly, the negative effects that you're probably seeing in your own business because of them. I also want to take this time to give you some further clarity on your business through a few short self-assessment questions. These will open your eyes to what is and isn't working in your business right now, and how you can start to improve things right away.

After that, I'm going to introduce you properly to the **Zero Leads** approach and hopefully show you why it's the answer to most of the struggles you're currently facing in your business. I also like to play "devil's advocate", so we're going to go through the main problems that people might face with the **Zero Leads** method, just to give you a balanced view.

We'll then dive into the entire **Zero Leads** framework, from start to finish. This is the exact same framework I use in my business personally and with all of my clients to dramatically increase their revenues while reducing their workloads.

Next, we're going to spend a while focusing on making those real, actionable changes in your business. We'll be looking at your **Signature Offers**, the first major part of the **Zero Leads** method. I'll show you how to develop your **Unique Framework**, how to split that into different priced products and services across the value spectrum, and finally how to get your first great product ideas that your potential clients won't be able to resist.

By the end of this book, you'll not only have a much deeper understanding and appreciation of the **Zero Leads** method, but you'll also have your entire offer strategy complete.

Finally, we'll look at how you can package up your offers to get as many of your ideal clients buying them as possible. I'll lay out the skills you'll need and the hires you should make to build out your own product and sales development teams. I'll also let you know a bit more about how my team and I can help you grow your business using the method outlined throughout this book.

Now when you lay it out like that, it seems like a lot to go through, but in all honesty, the whole of this book can be summed up in **3 simple points**:

- **Point #1:** Spending time and money on acquiring leads is inefficient and is harming the profitability of your business.

- **Point #2:** Only when you start focusing on acquiring customers will you be in a profitable position, ready to grow.

- **Point #3:** The best method to acquire ideal, new customers is the one you'll find in this book - The **Zero Leads** method.

The method you're about to discover has led to a massive transformation in my life, not only from a business perspective, but also on a personal level too. It's opened up a door to financial and social freedom I never thought I'd have. I truly do hope that you'll find your own freedom with this method also.

On the face of it, this book is about sales and marketing, but I have also been in business for a very long time and have learned a lot over the years (usually the hard way!). I didn't just want this book to be all process, so you'll also find some of the most valuable lessons I've had the privilege of learning at points throughout the book.

Business is as much about mindset as it is about strategy and tactics. **The more we can strengthen our mindset, the more easily we can succeed in everything else.**

This book has literally been 15 years in the making. It's something that I've worked on one-to-one with clients for years but wanted to get it out to the world. I've been excited to write it and I'm excited for you to read it. It's a real honour to share this with you and I hope it inspires and motivates you to improve your own business so you can improve your life and the lives of those around you.

If at any point throughout this book you decide you'd like help implementing any part of the strategies as quickly as possible, please book a call with me and my team by going here:

www.growthquadrant.co/call

We're passionate about helping people like you design a profitable business that can scale and grow to where you want it to be. Whether that's sitting very comfortably at 5-figure months or shooting for a multiple 7-figure machine, we're here to help.

Let's start growing your business!

James Bray

PART 1
PERSPECTIVE SHIFT

1
EARN MORE, BE MORE

"Free your mind. Free your body. Free your soul. Free yourself from the trappings of the mundane, the doubt, and the expected. There is more in us. There is more in you. The world expects conformity. To fit into the mould it sets for us. We are more than that. You are more than that. It's time to break the mould. Strive to live in happiness. Live to give happiness to others. Be who and what you want to be. There is only one mould. The one we set for ourselves."

--

I want to show you what life could be like for you using the **Zero Leads** method.

When I started focusing all my time and efforts on paying customers instead of hustling for leads, I suddenly saw a massive shift in the day-to-day running and overall success of my business. **This "re-focus" literally changed everything.**

I could finally say goodbye to those time-wasting, bottom-of-the-barrel clients. You know the ones; the clients that haggle your rates down, that don't understand, appreciate or respect your skill and expertise. The clients that micro-manage and treat you like they know best. The clients that keep shifting the goal posts, that want more and more, but aren't willing to pay more. And the clients that don't even pay at all. That you have to constantly chase just to get your due payment of the hard work and effort you've put into their businesses.

I now only work with my ideal clients. I get to pick and choose. The clients that I work with are already pre-qualified before I even talk to them. They already spend money with me before I even talk to them. They know exactly who I am, what I can do for them and, more importantly, precisely what they want my team and I to help them with. I don't need to chase and hassle potential clients. They come to me because they know I can help them.

And for me, that's what makes me happy. Knowing that I'm helping those that want to help themselves. Knowing that I can help people who are serious about changing their lives and finding success and happiness in their own business.

In this book, **I'm going to show you how you can also go from a "lead-hustler" to a "client-magnet"**. I'm going to show you the very simple process of building trust and belief in others so that when they see your $10,000+ services, they'll think them "cheap" for the value they get from them.

I also don't lose money acquiring new customers. In fact, I make a profit on my ad spend alone. This is something else I'm going to show you how to setup in your business in a later chapter. Marketing is no longer an expense (as it is in so many businesses). Every activity I do in my business has a positive ROI (Return On Investment). For every dollar I put into something (either of my money or my time) I get more than one dollar back.

That's the *true* secret to unlocking the growth potential in any business!

I've also cut out a lot of the activities in my business that were not making me money - everything that had a negative ROI. And this is where I've seen the biggest impact. I now only work 2 days a week. The rest of the time I'm able to spend with my family, playing with my two young daughters and taking time to look after myself, being able to exercise and relaxing my mind. All the "rewards" of freedom, purely because of the security and stability that my business offers me.

For me, that's the most important thing. Freedom. Money's a great asset to have, but it's only a means to an end. Nobody wants money, just to have money. They want money for the doors it opens. And the most important door we have to open is time.

Time is the most important asset we have, because it's finite. We can always make more money. We are always losing time. So, to be able to be free in your time. To be in full control of your time. Of how you spend it, where you spend it, who you spend it with. That is the true beauty and power of this method.

The method itself is nothing ground-breaking. There are no "Nobel Prize-winning", generational leaps in thinking. The method is simple. And ironically, it's because of its simplicity that it's little-used. We tend to think that more is better. That complexity delivers better results, but it's actually the other way round. **Simplicity is the secret to scale.**

It's easy to constantly add more and more. To throw anything and everything together and see what sticks. Simplicity is the hard part. Reducing something down to its most efficient form. Zero waste. That's where the magic lies. And that's where freedom begins.

Because of my constant drive for simplicity, I can keep my business profitable, fun and easy to run.

I don't need to constantly be giving away my content. I don't need to be everywhere on social media. I don't need to be on job boards. I don't need to run sales pitches disguised as "free webinar training". I don't need to add forced urgency with fake countdown timers and "limited seats" to my offers. I don't need to manage a massive team. I don't need to drive myself into the ground by trying to stay on top of every latest sales and marketing tactic, trick and hack. And it's all thanks to the method you're going to learn about in this book.

I spend less than thirty minutes a day "marketing" my business because I've built an automated machine that's profitable from the outset. A machine that's working for me 24 hours a day, 365 days a year. If I'm doing project work, it's getting me customers. If I'm sleeping, it's getting me customers. If I chose to go on holiday for a month, it'll still be getting me customers. Money will still be coming into my business. If I stop working, it doesn't.

Over the following pages, I'll give you the overall structure and strategies of the **Zero Leads** method so you can see how it could bring you the solid, consistent and profitable results you've been looking for to grow your business and improve your life.

The only way to know for sure is to read through this book, from cover to cover. It's not a long book. I've purposefully kept it short so that it's easy to read. My goal is not for you to read my book. My goal is for you to understand the method and start applying it in your business as quickly as possible to get the results you want and deserve.

Are you ready to begin?

Let's do it!

2
WHO THIS BOOK (AND METHOD) IS FOR

"Our existence is defined by actions, not words. Those who say and don't do quickly lose the respect of others. All hat and no cattle. Words lose meaning when they're backed by emptiness. We're judged on what we do. Day in, day out. And it's what we do that makes us who we are. Who we're seen to be. Reality has no patience for "I would've...", "I should've...", and "I was gonna...". Reality only cares for what is. Whether you like it or not, you are what you do. And if you don't like who you are, it's time to do something different..."

--

The **Zero Leads** method has definitely led to the happiest times of my life, but it hasn't always been that way. I don't want to drag you down fully into the "dark hole" I was living in, but the choices I'd made a few years before had led me to the worst times in my life.

I'd been in the corporate world for my whole working life. From the outside it probably looked like I had it going pretty good. Managing the Sonic The Hedgehog brand across the world in over 30 different countries. Negotiating international brand expansions for a well-known vitamins brand. Rolling out a complete re-brand for the world's

#1 baby swimming school in the UK, Europe, Canada, China and Australia. I was heading up my own marketing team. I was taking home over $70,000 / year. I was comfortable. But I was miserable. I was stressed. I was working 15-hour days (plus weekends) and had zero freedom.

My eldest daughter was born in 2015. That was when it hit me. That "time" was truly my most valuable and precious asset. Time to be with her and my wife. Then two years later, we had a double whammy, the pure excitement of our second daughter being born, and the utter devastation when we were also told, out of the blue, that our eldest daughter had Cerebral Palsy. Those three events in my life cemented the desire in me to be in full control of my time. To be free to choose how I spend it.

So, I quit my job and started freelancing.

And it was tough. I don't think I realised what I'd gotten myself into. I had definitely bitten off more than I could chew and was very quickly burning through the little savings that we had. I had such a desire to make it work that I ended up working more than I did in my full-time jobs.

I blindly threw myself into my work thinking the more I dedicated myself to it, the more time I spent on it, the more things I did for it would mean the more successful it would be. I had given up so much, my family needed me to succeed, I *had* to make it happen.

But the more I hustled my way through it, the further from success I got. I wasn't thinking. I was just doing. I couldn't see that I was doing more and more of the wrong thing. I was making it too complicated. I was wasting my time and money on every activity.

The amount of stress I put on myself was immense. So much so that I fell into deep depression. I was neglecting myself and my family. I wasn't even earning enough money for food and bills. I was failing miserably. I hated my business. I felt like a failure. My confidence had hit rock bottom. I was having panic attacks about the future. I was receiving therapy. My diet was terrible, and I was putting on a lot of weight. My marriage was realistically a few weeks away from being over.

In the end I had to sell my car to pay the bills. But more embarrassingly, I "admitted defeat" and went back to a full-time job selling fork-lift trucks. I was back in that miserable world again, but at least I could financially support my family.

Funnily enough, it was the thing that had caused so much pain in my life that set me free from it. My daughter's Cerebral Palsy. By nature of the condition, she finds it difficult to walk, her balance is majorly affected, and she falls over a lot. But every time she fell over, she would get back up again. It would be a struggle to get to her feet, but she would do it. Because she had to.

And I knew what I had to do. I had fallen over, but I was choosing to stay down. I was a failure. Because I was refusing to get back up. So, I got up.

Her strength, determination and wilfulness inspired the same in me.

I got up.

I started to read and learn. I knew a lot about sales and marketing already, it was my profession, but I wanted to know more. I wanted to find a solution to where I'd been going wrong. I systematically went through every single activity I did and removed the complexity. I simplified everything. I honed everything down into the most effective, efficient activities and generating profit for the least effort possible.

I wanted my time back. I wanted my happiness back. So, I ploughed every waking minute I wasn't "working" into creating a new method. A method that would set me on the path to my own freedom. A method that would ultimately become the **Zero Leads** method that this book is about.

In 2019, I started this business, **Growth Quadrant**. I tested what I had learned - my new framework on my own business until it started delivering the results I wanted.

I was finally there!

A method that continues to give me the gift of both time and money.

I'm no longer stressed by working long hours. I'm no longer anxious about what the future holds. I've got over my depression and regained my self-belief and confidence. I look after my mental and physical wellbeing. I'm there for my children. And I get to work with awesome clients that are passionate about making a real difference in their own businesses and lives.

I don't feel the pressure of having to work with anyone that throws a bit of money at me because "I don't know when I might get another client" or "I've got bills to pay".

What I'm going to be teaching you in this book will set you on the path of achieving these things in your life. It may be a business system for generating revenue, but **the knock-on effects reach much further than your business alone.**

When you have more money, you have the luxury of more time. And with more time comes more control. You free yourself up to become a force for *good* in the world. You have time to deliver more value and help those around you achieve more.

I sincerely believe it's our obligation as human beings to enhance the lives of others and make this world a better place for ourselves and for our children. For everyone to live their lives in a state of abundance.

If you don't feel like you have that yet, I want you to keep reading. Massive transformation starts with *simple* changes. And it's this simple method that could be the catalyst for you.

By following the method laid out in this book, you'll be able to attract your ideal clients on autopilot, build a solid foundation of trust between you, fill your pipeline with clients and projects you're excited to work with/on, and see a seismic shift in the amount of revenue your business generates.

I'm going to introduce you to the art of simple. To remove the complexities in your sales process and focus solely on the handful of things that will grow your business.

If you're a creative freelancer with the motivation to grow, this method has specific and unique benefits for you. Being of "service" to someone is the purest, most personal form of helping them, and this method will allow you to help more people than you've ever dreamed of.

Key Takeaways:

- Hustle and complexity are the destroyers of profitability and growth. If you want to make more money, you need to make things more simple. Where there's simplicity, there's less stress, confusion and effort. Where there's complexity, there's less efficiency and more chance of something going wrong.

- Money is purely an exchange for freedom. The more money we have, the more freedom we have. The freedom of choice and control. The freedom to give to and enhance the lives of others, without holding anything back.

- It's our moral obligation as human beings to help those around us and ultimately make the world a better place for ourselves and our children. Everyone deserves to live in a state of abundance.

3
THE 5 BARRIERS TO PROFITABLE GROWTH

"To fail is to learn. To fail is to understand. To fail is to progress. To fail is to be in a better position than we were before we started. We've not lost anything. We've gained something precious. We've gained insight from our own direct experience. We've gained insight specific to our unique situation. Failure is not the end. It's the beginning. Great success is built on a mountain of small failures. Learn to fail well. Heed the lessons from your failures. Embrace their teachings and move on from them. What you may lose is temporary. What you gain is eternal."

--

I've helped businesses grow their customer numbers and bottom-line profits since 2003. I've worked with both massive global brands and small startups and freelance business owners.

Every time I start working with a company, **I see the same mistakes being made again and again**. The same mistakes that block their ability to grow past the point they're currently at. And it's funny, the size of the business doesn't matter, these mistakes are universal. You'd think that the massive, household-name brands would have it all figured out, but in all but the rarest of cases, there are still things they fall short on - and by quite a margin!

To be completely honest with you, I've even been accountable for some, if not all of these mistakes in my time. With other people's businesses and my own. I've done things to prevent the growth of companies I've worked for and companies I've owned. I've learned the hard way in a lot of these cases. It's so easy to make these mistakes. That's the very reason they're so widespread. But it's also very easy to fix them…

There are a lot of mistakes I've either made or seen over my 15+ year career, but I've managed to condense them down into 5 main areas. I call them the **5 Barriers To Profitable Growth** and I want to share them with you. For two reasons really:

So that you don't make the same mistakes in your business.

To show you why I'm so obsessed with the **Zero Leads** approach to growing service businesses to 7-figure a year assets, and beyond.

With that said, let's dive into the valuable lessons you can use in your business to avoid the common pitfalls to growth:

Barrier #1: No Client Focus

This is the most common problem I've seen across the years, and it isn't going away any time soon, unfortunately.

Too many businesses are inward facing. They're fully focused on themselves, they only talk about themselves, they're so "in love" with their own products, services and story they forget about their actual customers and clients.

Another failing is not having a defined target audience to go after at all. **If you're aiming for everyone, you're going to get no-one.** In order to properly appeal to a certain type of customer/client, you need to know everything about them. You can't know everything about a million different types of people, that's why it's best to choose one and go *deep*.

I was working for a major international brand developing a re-brand strategy for them a few years back. The first thing I asked them (and the first thing I ask anyone I work with) was about their customers.

Now when I say "about" their customers, I mean *everything* about their customers. I want to know their wants, pains, desires, challenges, objections, feedback, thoughts, feelings, behaviours, lifestyle etc. To me this is basic, standard stuff.

If you don't know everything about who you're trying to work with/sell to, how do you know you're giving them the best value you can and the type of value they most want?

I was sent a PowerPoint file that had a *single* slide in it (that always sets alarm bells ringing…). It had details of their age range, family status and annual household income. *That was it.* This was an international business turning over tens of millions of dollars a year, and the only thing they knew was how old their customers were! Crazy!

It was no wonder that as their first-mover advantage was starting to wear off and competition was starting to ramp up, they were seeing a stagnation in new customers coming into the business.

After doing some digging, I found that they had a testimonial system setup, but no-one had even logged in in *over 4 years*! There was a gold mine of information, directly from their customers there, that wasn't even being used.

I also set up the biggest customer and non-customer survey that went to over 100,000 of their ideal targets to get a much deeper insight into *who* their customers actually were and what their *drivers* were. That alone fed into a massive redevelopment of their website, sales systems, offers and services, along with the complete rebrand.

Now everything was based on their customers. Not the business owners.

This raises a very important point I want to make...

People don't care about you and your business. They care about themselves.

The more you talk about you, the more you'll lose them. The more you talk about them, the more they'll gravitate towards you.

Everything you do needs to have your customers and clients in mind. **Everything you do should make their lives easier, better and more enjoyable.**

A great way of testing this is to look at how you talk to your potential clients. If you're using "I" and "we" more than "you" and "your", then you have an inward-facing problem.

There're 2 parts to fixing this problem. The first is to obviously learn a lot more about your potential clients. The second is to design everything in your business around them, not you.

The **Zero Leads** method that you'll be learning about in this book has been created to do just that. In fact, *Chapter 11* is completely devoted to finding out more about your potential ideal clients so you can start positioning your business around helping them fully.

Reality Check Assessment:

I didn't want this book to be just something you read, I wanted it to be something that helps you see positive results *right now* also. For each of the **5 Barriers**, I've created **Reality Check Assessments** so you can get a clearer picture of where you are in your business right now.

Go through each of the statements on the next page and score yourself on a scale of 1-5 at how strongly you agree with them, 1 being "not at all", 5 being "strongly agree".

Once you've added up your score, take a look at the next section for my personal, tailored recommendations to start improving your business.

Reality Statement	Score
I have a defined "ideal client persona" that I use when marketing my business.	
I fully understand my clients' wants, needs, pains, challenges, objections, values and motivations.	
I built my brand around my ideal clients' preferences, not my own.	
I use "you" and "your" more than "I", "we" and "our" when speaking to potential clients.	
My services are designed to make my clients' lives as easy and enjoyable as possible.	
I have an automated system in place for easily collecting client testimonials.	
My clients are more than willing to provide case studies about the results they've achieved with my business.	
I regularly survey my clients and target audience to find out more about them and what they need.	
I constantly listen in to communities and forums to keep up with the latest trends with my clients.	
I ask my potential clients questions first and give "solutions" after, rather than the other way round.	
Your Total:	

What Your Score Means

Score: 1-24: Narrow Your Focus

You have most likely set up a service based on what "you" can do - your skills and abilities, but not thought how those abilities could help benefit a specific audience. You'll find yourself "pitching" your services to whoever will listen but coming off as generic and not winning a lot of project work.

It's time to start focusing on a specific type of client. Clients that you want to get to know, understand and help. You already have the ability to help them, you just need to home in and stop aiming to grab anything that shows the least bit of interest in your business.

One of the most fundamental exercises of the **Zero Leads** method is to know a very specific target audience inside-out, and work to attract and help them. The narrower you go, the more you'll grow.

Score: 25-36: Enhance The Relationship

You've got your target ideal client in mind, you probably know their basic demographic information (age, gender, location, business type, annual revenue etc). You talk about some of their pain points and how you can help them. The fact that you're honing down on an audience means that you're starting to win more contracts from being more specific.

Your best plan of action now is to start looking at your relationship-building process. You know who they are, it's time to start bonding with them and building higher levels of trust.

In *Chapter 6* of this book, we'll go into how you can start achieving that with the **Zero Leads** method. As people trust you more, they work with you more and *pay* you more.

Score 37+: Scale The Relationship

You're smashing it with your current target audience. You know exactly who you're talking to. You know what makes them tick and how you can position your services to help them. And you're building trusting, profitable relationships with them.

Now it's time to automate and systemise the processes you have built in your business so you can scale out your relationship-building efforts to more of your ideal clients at once. As part of the **Zero Leads** method, I'll show you exactly how that's possible - and with less work and effort on your part than you're putting in now.

Barrier #2: No Offer Strategy

Service businesses are generally notoriously *poor* at defining a profitable offer strategy. They'll usually have their main service and that's about it.

That service will be offered to everyone, no matter their circumstances, and altered on the fly depending on what the potential client can afford. It won't be a systematic, strategic decision, it'll be a one-off change of plans to accommodate their needs.

There are 2 *very* large issues with this:

Not every potential client you come across might be ready for your single premium service. In fact, they might not be ready for one-to-one help at all.

If you're having to start from scratch for every single client that comes along, you're unnecessarily wasting a lot of time and money changing small things here and there for not a lot of extra return.

Not having a system of offers will mean that you'll be missing out on potential clients that are looking for the overall result you provide, just delivered in a different way. It also means that **your life is going to be much more stressful as you try and create a unique service every single time.**

Imagine if Nike created shoes that were specifically designed to every person's feet that bought them. Not only is that way too complex to scale, but it'll probably also destroy their business, especially at the prices they currently charge.

When deciding our offers, we need to stop thinking in terms of products and services, but in overall results delivered.

We're going to do a deep dive into your offer strategy in *Chapters 9 and 10*, where I'll take you through the exact steps to create solid, profitable offers for your business.

In the meantime however, I just want to briefly introduce you to the main solution to this, and that's **productisation**.

Productisation essentially means taking your service and breaking it into repeatable, scalable chunks that you can offer for every client, without any alterations. Each of those "chunks" can be different to each other, but they'll always be delivered in the same way.

When you design your services in such a systematic way, a few magical things happen. You'll then be able to predict with great certainty the effort involved for yourself and your team, the cost of delivering a project, the time it'll take to deliver it and the exact number of projects you can deliver within any particular time frame.

It turns a once "chaotic" business, where you're constantly trying to grasp some form of control, into **a predictable, well-oiled machine that you can easily scale.**

It also turns out that most people don't want bespoke, tailored services - not in the way you think anyway. Yes, they want it to be unique to their business, but as for the system that delivers results, they want something that's been proven time and time again to work.

Think about it, would you rather have a car that's a prototype, one-off that hasn't been test driven before, or a car that's had a few million units built and tested over the last two years to the point where all the issues have been ironed out?

You'll still probably want to personalise it by buying it in your favourite colour, maybe with the extra sound system and entertainment setup, (which, by the way have also been produced countless times over in the same way) but you'll want the underlying engine and chassis to have a proven history of quality.

The **Zero Leads** method is founded on the idea of great offer design. As mentioned, we'll be sorting out your **Signature Offer** later in this book, but for now, let's see where you currently stand in your business around your offer strategy:

Reality Check Assessment:

Go through each of the statements below and score yourself on a scale of 1-5 at how strongly you agree with them, 1 being "not at all", 5 being "strongly agree".

Once you've added up your score, take a look on the next page for my personal, tailored recommendations to start improving your business.

Reality Statement	Score
I don't just rely on a single service offer for my business revenue.	
I have a strict system and processes in place to deliver my services.	
I'm able to accurately predict the time, effort and cost it will take to complete all the projects I take on.	
I'm confident of the exact results I can achieve on every project.	
I can deliver my services to clients without being stressed and frustrated.	
I run my project work in the most efficient, effective ways possible.	
I know the exact amount of project work I can take on in a month.	
I can accurately predict the people and resources I would need to scale my service offer.	

I have a unique service/framework that sets me apart from my competition.	
I'm completely happy and confident in the results and value I deliver to my clients.	
Your Total:	

What Your Score Means

Score: 1-24: You Need A Framework

With a score this low, things a probably very chaotic for you. The projects that you take on will change each and every time with no two projects the same. You're pretty much doing it all on the fly. This is costing you time, money and your sanity.

What you need is stability. You need systems and processes in place that you can work through like clockwork which will always deliver the same result at the end for each and every client. You need predictability to stop your head from exploding.

Take a look at the **Signature Offer** section in this book. The first chapter in that section (*Chapter 9*) will take you through everything you need to define your own **Unique Framework** that you can roll out and perfect for every client you work with. The **Zero Leads** method is all about structure and stability. Everything needs to be simple so you can scale it and grow.

Score: 25-36: Expand Your Offers

You've probably got your main service offer down. You've got a specific set of systems and processes you use to deliver it and your clients are getting a pretty standardised service and set of results off the back of it. You're almost living in the comfort zone, but not pushing yourself much.

That's the problem here though, you're leaving money on the table elsewhere. With just one service offer type, you're only hitting one type of client. In the **Zero Leads** method, we work on hitting all 3 main client types by creating specific offers for all of them. We'll go through exactly what those offers need to be in *Chapter 10* a bit later on.

Score 37+: Step Away From Delivery

You're the "offer expert". You're literally covering all bases with the offers you have and hitting each of your client types with solutions they need, when they need them. You're even probably using your smaller, initial offers to drive more clients into your more premium offers to increase your revenue and profit levels.

You've probably started hitting a bit of a ceiling though. Because you're taking it all on, you don't have the resources to accept more project work. This is where you need to start scaling your offers by removing yourself from the equation and handing over to a dedicated team working for you.

The **Zero Leads** method enables you to start hiring pretty quickly due to the way the revenue generation is handled and the positive cash flow it yields. It's time to start thinking what you want to hand over and how you're going to do it.

Barrier #3: No Sales & Marketing System

A lot of the time, most freelancers take the approach of "show people my service...hope they buy it." Now there are two very valid parts of that approach. You definitely need to show people what you can offer them, and you also need them to buy it to grow your business. The one part of that whole "strategy" that's not ok however is the "hope" part.

Those that don't plan, hope. Those that do, get.

That's the general way things go. Now that's not to say that *any* old plan will get you what you want. But what any old plan will get you are results that you can systematically improve on until you mould it into the "right" plan.

And when you create a plan of action, you need a system of processes to carry out that plan effectively.

I've worked with a number of businesses whose plans stopped at "get customers". Well, that's quite an open and broad plan. There are a million and one different systems that you could implement to try and achieve that plan. And in most cases, that's exactly what they start doing.

They take a scattergun approach and literally start doing everything (but not doing anything particularly well). And how could they? To take on the entire "world" of marketing activity you need to have an incredibly huge strategy and an incredibly huge team to implement and monitor it. Most times it's around 1-3 people trying to do all of that. And in the case of solopreneur businesses, that one person is also the one that needs to deliver the projects and run the entire business!

It's no wonder that there's so much stress and burnout in the world of business. We're all easily distracted by "shiny things syndrome", the next best thing, the fear of missing out on what could be the "one thing" to launch our business into the stratosphere.

We take on *too much*!

It doesn't matter if were talking about the passionate "companies of one" or the goliath mega-brands of the world, we take on too much. We're on *every* single social platform, we're creating 57 blog posts a month, we're pumping out a video every minute on YouTube, we're streaming hours of podcasts...and we're killing ourselves doing it!

And the worst thing? In 99% of cases, we're not doing any of them that well! **When we spread our focus so thinly and overwork our capacity, we're bound to drop balls** - a lot of them. When we spend all our time doing, we don't have any time to take a step back and ask ourselves "why?". What's the purpose? Should we be doing this? Is there something better we could be doing? What is working for us the best and how can we do more of that?

Instead, we trap ourselves on the marketing hamster wheel and struggle to get off. Constantly trying to go forward when a simple side-step is all we need to slow down and regroup.

There are only **2 things** then that we need to have an effective sales and marketing process:

- A strategic plan

- An efficient system to carry out that plan

When we're talking about systems, the best systems in the world are automated as much as possible. There are huge advantages to doing this:

- More cost-effective

- Less manual effort needed

- Less room for human error

- More consistent experience for every client

- More scalable

- More predictable with the results they deliver

- Easier to analyse and report on

- Easier to hone and improve

All of this basically means that you get more and better results, for less effort and less cost. It also means you can take on more marketing activity without having to dedicate all your time to it.

That's the real beauty of building an automated marketing system.

The overall goal is to remove yourself as much as possible from it. **Ideally, you want the system to market your business and attract new customers and clients without any effort from you whatsoever.**

There are various ways to automate, including apps and tools, team hires and outsourcing. But ultimately a great system is dependent on great processes, and great processes are dependent on a great plan.

The **Zero Leads** method that we'll go into fully over the coming chapters combines the plan, processes and system you need to automate your marketing and sales activity. **I'm going to show you exactly what you need and how to set it up to start bringing new customers and clients into your business while you sleep**…literally.

So now, as with the last two Barriers, I'd like you to focus on your business in relation to this. Take a look at the statements below and score yourself as to where you think you are currently. Then take a look at the score results for recommended next steps:

Reality Check Assessment:

Go through each of the statements below and score yourself on a scale of 1-5 at how strongly you agree with them, 1 being "not at all", 5 being "strongly agree".

Once you've added up your score, see the following sections for my personal, tailored recommendations to start improving your business.

Reality Statement	Score
I have a specific plan for marketing my business and effectively attracting my ideal clients.	
I have systems and processes in place that automatically acquire new customers for my business.	
I have a select few "go-to" marketing channels where I focus my efforts that consistently deliver me new clients.	
I can accurately predict the number of new customers & clients my marketing efforts bring in each month.	
I am always "net-zero" on my marketing activity and gain my new clients without cost.	
My prospective clients all have the exact same, finely honed experience with my business before they start working with me.	
I personally spend only 15-30 minutes per day successfully marketing my business.	
I'm completely happy with the results that my marketing efforts give me.	
My marketing system always delivers top quality, pre-qualified clients that are ready and willing to work with me.	
I actively look to build real, trusting, profitable relationships with my potential clients even if they don't use my services initially.	
Your Total:	

What Your Score Means

Score: 1-24: Stop The Scattergun

You're probably spending a lot of time jumping to and from different tactics. A bit of LinkedIn here, a few Facebook/Insta posts there. But you're not seeing a lot of return on your efforts. Nothing's focused. You most likely see it all as a chore and a waste of time because it's not working. You try the "next best thing" a few times before giving up.

You need structure. You need to start focusing and dedicating your efforts on developing a system that takes potential clients from "just met" to "can't wait to work with you". That's exactly what the **Zero Leads** method is all about and the perfect system to start getting you out of the bad relationship you currently have with marketing your business.

Score: 25-36: Automate Your Processes

You likely have a number of marketing activities and channels in place that you use regularly and are getting ok results from them. You feel comfortable using them and you don't need to get distracted by "shiny object syndrome".

There's probably a feeling in the back of your mind that you could be doing better though, that you could be spending your efforts more effectively. Your marketing activity is taking a much larger percentage of your time than you would like.

It's time to turn those manual marketing processes into something that's more automated. You need your time back so you can focus on other areas of your business. The **Zero Leads** method will give you a tried and tested process for bringing new clients into your business on autopilot. You just need to "set and forget".

Score 37+: Shoot For The Stars

You have a finely honed and targeted marketing strategy that's working for your business. You have systems and processes in place that are successfully bringing in new clients at a fairly regular rate. Although you're still probably taking a lot of it on yourself.

Your next step is to scale up your efforts with less work on your part. Whether that's through completely automating your systems or hiring a team to help you expand your business, there are a wealth of options open to you using the **Zero Leads** method that can simplify your marketing activities, ready for scale.

Barrier #4: No Paid Traffic Strategy

A lot of freelance business owners are afraid to go anywhere near paid traffic.

They see it as a massive, risky investment where they'll probably lose money. "Facebook, Google and whatever new platform that may come along, are just there to take your money". And it's kind of hard to go against this school of thought when there are so many stories of businesses ploughing huge sums of money into paid ads and not getting anything for it. They blame "algorithm" changes, or "rising ad costs" that are "destroying" their ability to make money.

Well, it's true that there have been (and always will be) algorithm changes. But these changes are usually for the better. Yes, what may have once worked no longer works, but what now works, works even better…if you know how to take advantage of it properly.

It's also true that ad costs have risen (and always will). That's simply a fact of life and business. As ad platforms get more popular and demand increases, prices will increase along with it. It's basic economics. But that doesn't mean you can't make money from them anymore! You just need to adjust your tactics.

Let's think about it from the ad platform's point of view. If Facebook, let's say, increased ad prices to the point where no-one made any money anymore, no-one would buy Facebook ads anymore and Facebook would instantly lose all that revenue. That's hundreds of millions of dollars they would be "chopping" out of their business. Definitely not in their best interests to do that. It's in the ad platform's best interests to make it as effective as possible for businesses to make money. The more we make money, the more we buy ads, the more they make money.

The only reason that so many businesses lose money with paid ads is that they're doing it wrong.

It's as simple as that.

As with everything, there's a right way and a wrong way. And unfortunately, a lot of businesses enter the world of paid ads in the *wrong* way. They don't get the results they hoped for, and never return. Or worse yet, hear stories from other businesses going about it the wrong way and don't start in the first place!

Here's the bottom line, hard truth:

If you want to grow your business to 7-figures and beyond, you <u>need</u> to use paid traffic as part of your strategy to reach enough people to do it.

Blogging and posting on social isn't enough, not if you want to start growing now. Yes, it can be done organically, but it'll take much longer…many years longer. I'm not sure about you, but I'm not one for drawing something out when it can be done in a fraction of the time.

The problem is people get scared of ads because they don't know how to do them correctly.

The point I made previously has probably stuck with you throughout all of this. That ad costs are always rising. And you're probably thinking "well, if ads are getting more and more expensive, how do we actually make money from them?"

As part of the **Zero Leads** method, in *Chapter 7*, I'm going to show you exactly how you can incorporate paid traffic into your overall marketing strategy, for *free*. In most businesses, marketing activity is seen as an expense. I'm going to open your eyes to not only setup your paid traffic activity to pay for itself, but to also *profit* from it before you've even introduced your premium services!

For now though, how well do you currently incorporate paid traffic into your sales and marketing strategy?

Reality Check Assessment:

Go through each of the statements below and score yourself on a scale of 1-5 at how strongly you agree with them, 1 being "not at all", 5 being "strongly agree".

Once you've added up your score, take a look on the following page for my personal, tailored recommendations to start improving your business.

Statement	Score
I use paid traffic effectively to drive new clients into my business.	
I can turn my client acquisition on and off as I need depending on my available resources.	
I know my exact conversion rates on my marketing activity, and how much money I need to spend to get a certain number of new clients.	
I can instantly test new product ideas and get immediate feedback on their viability.	
I can easily cope with rising ad costs and turn a profit on my paid activity.	
Over 80% of my new clients come from paid channels.	
I have one revenue source that could easily scale to $100,000 a month.	
I could step out of my business for a month and my revenue levels wouldn't be affected.	
I outsource/hire in my paid ad management so I can focus on other areas of my business.	
I spend less than 2 hours a week on organic marketing activity.	
Your Total:	

What Your Score Means

Score: 1-24: Start Your Paid Traffic Journey

It's time to venture into the world of paid traffic. Stop relying solely on organic methods that take too long to create and are probably not getting you the level of results you'd like.

The **Zero Leads** method is the safest bet for your new paid traffic strategy because the cost of the ads themselves are offset by the initial order revenue (which we'll discuss in detail in *Chapter 7*). Everything has already been created and tested for you. You just need to plug it in to your business and get the results you want.

Score: 25-36: Time To Fine Tune

You're running paid ads currently and seeing some pretty decent results, but nothing ground-breaking. It's a great sign of potential. You have a good service, decent offer and a specific audience you're targeting. You probably have a few last things you need to tweak and refine until your ads really hit their stride.

As part of the **Zero Leads** method, one of the fundamental pieces of the puzzle is driving traffic at $0 cost. Imagine that in your business? How profitable would your paid ads be then?

Score 37+: Scale Your Traffic

You've got your paid traffic strategy comfortably working for you. The next step is ramping that up across multiple ad platforms to become the no.1 authority in your niche. You have the ability to confidently increase your ad spend to more than $1,000 / day and still see a positive return.

The **Zero Leads** method will enable you to do all of that and more so you can quickly accelerate the number of clients that are driven into your business. You'll be able to battle against rising ad costs and turn a profit on your ad spend.

Barrier #5: No Soul

Finally, I'm moving away from the tactical barriers into something a bit more general, but just as important.

In fact, I've regularly seen this Barrier cause much more damage than all the others combined!

A business that has no soul, no personality, no purpose or cause, no spark or no difference will be instantly ignored and quickly forgotten about. When a business has no soul, it's boring. And where there's boredom, there's apathy.

Apathy is the one thing you don't want your potential clients to feel!

It doesn't matter if you don't focus on your customer, you don't have a logical offer strategy, you don't have an automated sales and marketing system or you don't take advantage of paid traffic. To be honest, you could even be outstanding and have all those things in place. If you turn off potential clients at the very first contact with you, they won't progress any further with you for those tactics to be of use anyway!

I'm sure you've come across many "forgettable" businesses in your time. You know the ones, generic, stock photo, nonsense buzzwords, the same as all the other businesses in their niche etc. The ones that you've scrolled past their ads without a second thought, walked past their store without a second glance. The businesses that scream "I don't know who I really am!".

And if they don't know who they really are, how are they going to help you become who you want to be?

There's no attraction there. No intrigue. No desire to learn and understand more. And **this single thing harms so many businesses more than they know**.

I've implemented re-brands for a lot of clients in my time, both small and large, and the first thing I do is dig down to find their soul. That fire inside that drives them and differentiates them from others in their industry.

We're drawn to people and businesses that are unique, novel, impactful and stand for something. That have values and aren't afraid to share them. That have a vision and mission they're striving to make happen. That have personalities that are infectious.

Businesses are no different than people in this way. We want to get to know people that have souls that inspire us. Likewise, we're drawn to businesses with souls that do the same. I beg you, don't fall into the "generic trap". Find your own fire and carve out a place in this world for you and your business.

And remember, **you won't be everyone's cup of tea**. And that's ok. 10% of people will absolutely love you and what you stand for. 10% of people will hate you and think you're the most pointless thing ever. And 80% of people will be completely indifferent to you.

Focus on the 10% that love you. Share your soul with them, and they'll share theirs with you. That's how relationships are formed. And **every dollar ever made throughout the history of business was made because of a good relationship**.

Ultimately, the key to attraction lies in what you say and how you say it (both verbally and non-verbally). **The more fire, passion and confidence you can generate, the more likely you are to attract and entice your ideal clients**. We'll be talking about this in much more detail in *Chapters 6 and 7,* where we'll be looking at how to create instant trusting relationships with your ideal clients from the very first point they "meet" your business.

How well do you show the "soul" of your business?

Reality Check Assessment:

Go through each of the statements on this page and score yourself on a scale of 1-5 at how strongly you agree with them, 1 being "not at all", 5 being "strongly agree".

Once you've added up your score, take a look at the next section for my personal, tailored recommendations to start improving your business.

Statement	Score
I have an effective brand strategy that has been specifically developed for my business.	
All of my sales and marketing material look and feel consistent.	
I know my values, what I stand for and let my clients know too.	
I'm not afraid to promise my clients great results.	
I have a documented tone-of-voice guide that anyone could use to "sound" on-brand.	
I have a specific vision and mission I'm working towards in my business.	
I stand for a cause much bigger than the products and services I offer.	
I have a set of brand guidelines that any designer could use to create incredible artwork in the style of my business.	
I'm not afraid to be "me" in my business. I don't need to pretend to be anyone else.	
I take culture and brand fit very seriously when I take on new team hires.	
Your Total:	

What Your Score Means

Score: 1-24: Discover Your Soul

In all honesty, you're probably a bit all over the place in your business. You don't have a purposefully designed look and feel or personality to attract your ideal clients. Your "brand" has probably just fallen into place without any thought as you've created assets for your business, and it's hurting your ability to connect with great clients.

You need to go right back to basics and figure out who you are and what you stand for as a business. You then need to look at designing the look and feel of your business to match that to get quality and consistency running through everything you do. We'll talk about that in more detail in *Chapter 7*.

Score: 25-36: Introduce Your Soul

You have a pretty decent idea of who you are and have some consistency in your brand look and feel. Clients can sense quality there but may not be getting a majorly unique experience and flavour of you.

It's time to really tighten up your personality, tone of voice and look and feel so that they're working together seamlessly and are instantly recognisable as your business. A re-brand may be on the cards - nothing major, but enough to bring everything in line.

Score 37+: Share Your Soul With The World

You're really confident in who you are and what you represent. You have a defined brand style with distinct personality that you've worked on creating for your business. You give off a high perception of quality and resonate well with your potential clients on first impression.

Your job now is to get your brand in front of as many of your potential ideal clients as possible. The **Zero Leads** method is a simple, practical way of taking your brand and reaching as many people as possible at

$0 cost. That's the power of the system. And when you have your brand in the right place, it becomes much easier to get new clients at "break-even" or even make a profit on the initial interaction.

Key Takeaways:

Barrier #1: No Client Focus
When you don't focus fully on your clients, or worse, don't have a defined target client type you're after, you'll end up sounding generic and won't be able to really empathise with their wants and pains. If you want to help someone, you need to know everything about them. When we don't know who we're talking to, we end up talking about ourselves, because that's all we know. And that's the quickest way to alienate people from your business.

Barrier #2: No Offer Strategy
You can't survive with just one offer. You need to have a range of different offers at different price points that hit your potential clients at different parts in their buying cycle. 98% of people won't go for your premium offer right away. You need to prepare them for it, and having the right offer strategy in place will help with customer retention and increased revenue.

Barrier #3: No Sales & Marketing System
In order to successfully and consistently bring new customers and clients into your business, you need to have the right plan, processes and system in place to do so. Secondly, that system needs to be automated as much as possible so you can concentrate on other areas of your business. Ideally, you want your system bringing in revenue while you sleep.

Barrier #4: No Paid Traffic Strategy
If you want to transform your business into a 7-figure

business and beyond, then you need to include paid traffic in your strategy. Organic alone won't be enough. People are afraid of paid traffic because they do it wrong and waste their money. But there are "right" ways of doing it that not only cover your ad costs but can also turn a profit, before clients even see your premium offers.

Barrier #5: No Soul
Lifeless, generic, run-of-the-mill businesses, lose. Potential customers and clients pass them by and never return. If you want to attract more of your ideal clients, you need to show them your fire, your passion, your personality. You need to stand for something and have impact and momentum. No-one wants to be stuck with the boring kid at the party. Be *interesting*. Make their day!

4
WHY YOU DON'T NEED (OR WANT) LEADS IN YOUR BUSINESS

"There should always be something. Something of value. Something worthwhile. Something of equal trade for the effort you put in. When you work for nothing you devalue your work. You devalue yourself, your skills and your soul. There should always be something. You must decide what that something is. A fair trade. A respectful acknowledgement of who you are and what you do. Be wary of nothing masked as something. The worst kind of nothing. Stay true to yourself and always gain something."

--

So now we get into the crux of it. The entire premise of the book (and method).

When I first started my marketing career in 2003, one of my tasks for The Walt Disney Company was to look into implementing a CRM (Customer Relationship Management) system that would nurture customers (and potential customers) automatically and electronically. This was the very beginning of the email marketing revolution.

Since then, **email marketing has exploded, becoming the highest ROI marketing activity a business can do**. I'm sure you've heard the saying "the money's in the list". It's been one of the driving mantras over the past 20 years as businesses started to realise how much money they could actually make off of their contact lists.

Your contact list is the most important asset you have in your business. It's wholly owned by you. No-one can take it away from you. It's not built on another platform that could be shut down and lost forever. It's yours to do with as you please.

It should be filled with people that have actively signed up to hear from you, that are bought in to your ideals, values and methods. They have a strong interest in your products and services and how you can help them. They are the most likely people that will buy from you - that 10% that love you. A thriving community made up entirely of your ideal clients.

With that in mind then, I have a question for you...

If your list is the most precious asset you have, why would you want to fill it with shit contacts?

All the "marketing gurus" out there are pushing you to build your list as big as possible. They're working the law of percentages. Generally, in these situations, 2-3% of your list will buy from you. So of course, the bigger your list, the more people will buy, and the more money you'll make.

The race is then on to grow your list as big as possible. So, what are we told to do? Give away your knowledge and content for free. Produce free "lead magnets" to get as many leads as possible.

But there's the "chicken and egg" situation, you need to build a massive list to make that 2-3% count...but the reason you're only getting 2-3% is because of the *type* of list you're building.

Let's think about this for a moment...

You're essentially under-valuing yourself and your ability by enticing them for free. The barrier to entry is nothing. Anyone and everyone with even a passing interest in what you're giving away will sign up to get it, if you've positioned it well enough. But then what happens?

From the very first interaction with your business, you've subconsciously taught them to under-value your work. And what's more, the "gurus" then tell us to give more of our knowledge and content away for free. "Give away the farm" they shout. "That'll build trust". And when they trust you, they'll buy from you.

Yup. I agree that builds trust alright. They now trust that you'll keep giving away your knowledge and content for free. Because that's what you *do*. That's *who* you are. And in all honesty, it is. By that point you haven't shown them anything different.

And suddenly, once you've built all this "trust", you're told to pitch your offers. You're thinking "awesome, I've built all of this "goodwill" with them now, they're bound to take me up on this offer". But you know what they're thinking? "Whoa! Hang on a minute, this is the "free" guy! Where did this paid thing come from?? Not sure I'm ok with that. I'm just gonna stick around and wait for more of their free stuff."

That'll be 97-98% of your list that does that, **because you've trained them that way**.

And for those 2-3% that do buy, you're going to have to work hard to get them to part with their money. This is the point when we start seeing the fake urgency countdowns being rolled out. The "free training (actually $997 offer webinar sales pitch)" invitations. The "only 3̶ 2 spaces left!" nudge tactics.

People don't pay you based on their respect for your ability to help them. They pay you out of fear of missing out on a "deal".

So, let's add this up. First, we train them to under-value our work and ability to help them. Second, we lie to them and trick them to part with their money?

This whole standard "lead-generation" thing now isn't sounding like such a pleasant idea, is it?

I hope that's not sitting right with you. It definitely doesn't sit right with me. I want my potential clients to value my skills, abilities and the results I'm able to deliver in their businesses. Just like I value their skills, abilities and what their businesses have to offer.

I have the utmost respect for my potential clients. I respect their needs, their challenges, their decisions and their intelligence. The last thing I'd want to do is "trick" them into spending money. That's not a great solution for anyone. It leads to unhappy clients and bad feelings. And it also leads to refund battles and bad reputations.

I want clients to decide to work with me because I can add value to their business, not because I've threatened to take an offer away in 48 hours' time.

Every result we get from our business is down to the way we've designed it. Now that design could've been intentional. It could've also been something we weren't even thinking about. But everything happens for a reason, and **it's our job as business owners to design our businesses in a way that gets us the results we want**, in the way we want to get them.

What if there was a way to increase that 2-3% purchase rate to 100%?

What if we designed our businesses to *eliminate* "leads" entirely?

What if we purposefully designed our businesses to only work with *paying customers*?

Here are the top 5 benefits of choosing a **Zero Leads** strategy:

Benefit #1: No More Freeloaders

Freeloaders are a waste of your time, energy and money. They take, take, take and never give back. They'll happily sit on your list and subscribe to your social channels, but they'll never balance out that value back to you. They'll never become a client.

Your aim in business isn't to create as many "fans" as possible, it's to help as many clients as possible. We're not Instagram influencers, we're sharp and savvy business owners looking to help others achieve. And in return, we want our profits and businesses to grow.

Some may argue the "Reciprocity Rule", that psychologically, we feel like we owe someone if they've done us a favour (by giving us free stuff for example). But in these cases, I don't believe this to hold true.

The internet is a wholly different place to real life. People can hide behind their screens in anonymity. This "shield" massively affects our usual internal desire to reciprocate, especially when there's no personal contact with members of the business directly. It's because of this that people are happy to simply take and not give back. And it's these people you don't need in your life.

Not having a massive list isn't a problem either. Especially if that massive list is made up of freeloaders. You can easily clear $100,000 / month with a small list. Because that small list will be made up of better-quality clients. Clients that convert at 40-50% into your premium products and services rather than 2-3%.

Benefit #2: Guaranteed Commitment

How many free things have you signed up for in the past? Now how many of them have you actually used? That's the problem with "free", it requires zero commitment. But as soon as you pay for something, you're pretty much guaranteed to use it. You've made a commitment to yourself and to the thing you've bought. You don't want to waste money, right?

Those that are willing to spend money from the very beginning to get a desired result are the ones that are truly serious about achieving it.

They're making a statement, even if it's only a small amount of money, it's still a massive psychological commitment and a massive indicator of their determination to improve.

And at the end of the day, aren't they the sort of clients that you want to be working with? The ones that actively work with you to achieve success. The ones that will be great case studies for your business. The ones that will attract other, like-minded businesses to you to help them achieve similar results?

Benefit #3: Customers Buy More

I'm sure you've heard the statistic that **it's 5x easier to sell something to someone that's already bought from you** than to someone that hasn't before?

Well, there's a lot of truth in that.

The success rate of selling to a current customer can be anywhere from 40-60%, however selling to a new customer is only around 5-20%.

That's a massive difference! And it's mainly down to 2 factors:

The first is an increase in trust. They've trusted you already with their money and time, and if you deliver the results they're looking for, they'll have no hesitation in trusting you again. Just like moving a boulder, it takes a lot of effort to get it moving, but once it is, it's easy to build momentum.

The second is what's known as the **Consistency Principle**. According to *Robert Cialdini* in the incredibly awesome book, *Influence: The Psychology Of Persuasion*, when we make a commitment to doing something, we have a natural tendency to behave in a way that's consistent with our original commitment. Put simply, if we begin by buying from a business, we're much more likely to continue buying from that business (unless the business gives them reason not to). We have an internal drive to be (and look) consistent with what we've already done in order to maintain "face" with others (and with ourselves). In other words, we don't really want to admit that our original action was the wrong choice.

We can see this in action when we talked about training your list. If the first interaction you have is something for free, then there's a much higher likelihood that the "free" trend will continue. **If it's an initial payment, then you've set the stage for the client to continue in a payment mindset.**

Benefit #4: Massively Reduced Costs

"Leads" are expensive.

If we're putting two and two together, we now know that it costs 5 times as much to acquire a new customer than it does to sell more to an existing one. We also know that attracting "leads" through the use of "free" lead magnets preps them towards a mindset and continued behaviour of "free".

These two obviously don't add up!

The biggest cost in your business will be acquiring new customers. Not just in the actual cost of paid advertising, but also in your own time and that of any team members you have helping you. When you put all of those together and you're aiming for that 2-3% of a "majority-freeloader" list for your revenue, you can see that the numbers are stacked *massively* against you.

And it's not only acquisition costs, but also the cost of keeping them. The more email contacts you have, the more emails you'll need to send, and the more your email platform will charge you for the privilege. For example, an engaged list of 1,000 customers will cost anywhere between $50-100 a month to maintain. Compare that to a list of 10,000 freeloaders (which would probably deliver you around the same amount of revenue), and you're looking at around 3-6 times that cost. That's already thousands of dollars you'd save! Again, all fine if you're successfully monetising your list properly, even a small one. But when you're battling with those 2-3% figures, it's going to be very hard covering your costs, let alone making a profit to grow your business and live the life you want.

As soon as you start focusing on a **Zero Leads** strategy however, every contact that you acquire is a paying customer. That income will already more than cover the cost of acquiring them in the first place (something we'll look at in much more detail in *Chapter 7*). The rest of the money you make from further sales with those existing customers is pure profit!

Your sales and marketing activities are now no longer expenditures in your business. They're either "break-even" or "profit-driving".

Benefit #5: You Can Grow

Once you have a sales and marketing system that delivers you new customers, 24/7, 365 days a year, and it doesn't cost you a thing (and might even make a profit), you'll have all the necessary foundations in place to rapidly grow your business.

If you know that no matter how much you "spend" on getting new customers into your business, it's free, then the sky's the limit. That's when you can throw $100,000 a month into paid traffic and get it all back before those new customers have even purchased your main services.

That's the true power of the **Zero Leads** system. And these are the exact benefits you'll see in your business when you start using it. And I know this, because they're the exact same benefits I see in my business every day. The **Zero Leads** method has been specifically designed to get you filling your contact lists with 100% customers as quickly as possible.

Throughout the rest of this book, you'll see the entire method laid out, so you understand everything about it. **By the end of this book, you'll know exactly what you need to do to design your business for maximum profit, not maximum headache.**

But before we go any further into the **Zero Leads** method itself, I wanted to balance out my views for you. I'm not here to preach my ideas as gospel. They're simply a result of my own business success and that of the clients I've helped. There's always another side to any story. I want you to decide and agree for yourself if the **Zero Leads** method is relevant for your business.

So, in the next chapter, I'll go through the counterargument and what the #1 *problem* is with a **Zero Leads** approach.

5
THE #1 PROBLEM WITH A ZERO LEADS APPROACH

"The greatest skill we have is the ability to understand. To truly understand. To put ourselves in the shoes of others. To walk their paths. To feel their joys. Their pains. Their fears. Their desires. It goes beyond the surface and mere facts. Beyond the false niceties and selfish agendas. Empathy is wholly selfless. Your world becomes theirs, for no other reason than understanding. And only when we understand, can we help. To sell is to empathise. You aren't selling what you want to sell. You're selling what they want to buy."

--

Now don't get me wrong, a 100% customer approach can be very risky.

Time and time again I see freelancers running ads straight to call booking forms, or driving cold traffic straight to their $997 programs. The number of paying clients they actually get from doing this is pitifully low, and I can guarantee you they aren't covering their ad costs.

Going straight for the sale can be one of the quickest ways to lose a lot of money, especially if you're paying for traffic. And even if you're not paying for ads and you're trying to drive traffic organically through social or search, that's still your time you're wasting. **And your time isn't cheap.** Your time is much better used for profitable client project work, not trying to constantly get people to your booking/order page.

This is a classic example of "asking for marriage on the first date". And to be honest, I would even argue that it's before the first date!

When you're looking to build a list of potential clients, traditional thinking is to try and attract as many people as possible. Everyone preaches about the need of having a big list you can pitch your services to. When you're giving stuff away for free, you'll most definitely start growing a big list. Everyone loves free stuff. But **if you're aiming for paying customers from the offset, your list will always be much smaller**. Your reach will be smaller.

And if you're going for that premature marriage sale, then you'll be lucky if you build any form of list at all.

So, if it makes it much harder to build a massive list of potential clients, which it does, why am I such an advocate of it?

The reason's quite simple really…

All these businesses are doing it wrong.

Just creating a premium service and driving traffic to a booking page is an insane business strategy. Most people don't know who you are, or care, and will definitely not turn into paying clients from an ad they didn't want and an order form they don't feel they need.

No-one wants to marry anyone they've literally just met. So why would it be any different in business? The service that you offer is your big, shiny wedding ring and all the commitment that comes with it. Now that's scary unless you're ready for it!

Business owners try the "big pitch" and fail, so instead turn to the "easiest" option by giving away their content and knowledge for free. They think that if they do that, they'll reach more people, and out of those "more people" they'll hopefully get more clients. They go from trying to pitch 4 & 5-figure services off the bat, to suddenly giving away stuff for free to try and get people to spend 4 & 5 figure amounts for their services. It makes no sense…

A premium offer alone makes no economic sense to filter new prospects to. But when it's part of a system containing a series of offers that meets the customer where they are in their buying journey, you'll find that's the quickest way to growing a business to 7-figures a year or more.

That's the key difference.

The #1 problem with a "no leads" approach is that it's completely useless without a system for developing customers and clients specifically at each stage of their buying journey. For us, that's the **Zero Leads** method you'll learn more about in this book. Without that system, a "no leads" approach will massively harm your business.

As you've seen up to this point from our time together, a **Zero Leads** approach can radically transform everything you do in your business. From the quality of the calls you have with prospective clients to your ability to increase your pricing (and levels of profitability).

But all of that assumes that you can get enough customers from the beginning in a way that doesn't lose you money and bankrupt your business.

So therefore, we have a bit of a problem to solve…

How do we attract as many paying customers as possible without losing money upfront?

We know that filling our contact lists with customers that have already paid for our help are significantly easier and more likely to turn into premium clients, but how do we get them to spend money with us in the first place and get past the "marriage at first sight" issue?

In the next chapter, we're going to start looking into the entire underlying philosophy behind the **Zero Leads** system, and then in *Chapters 7 and 8*, we're going to explore the **Zero Leads** system in detail for how you turn someone you've just met into an ideal, five-figure client.

Key Takeaways:

- Don't fall into the trap of "marriage at first sight" pitching. It's a sure-fire way of losing money and driving your business into the ground.

- A **Zero Leads** approach however is one of the most profitable changes you can make in your business, if done correctly. It can completely transform the quality of clients you bring in and the amount they're willing to pay for your services.

- Your premium service offer alone isn't enough to grow your business. It needs to be part of a system and combination of offers that meets your potential clients where they are and prepares them upfront to buy your premium services.

PART 2
THE ZERO LEADS FRAMEWORK

6
THE MARBLE RUN

"They're not your audience. They're not your clients. They're not your partners. They're not your associates. They're not your job. They're not your project. And they're not your paycheck. They are your family. Love them as such. Hate them as such. But they are your family. Be there for them like you would your own. Respect them. Care for them. Truly know them. Build a relationship beyond business. Make it personal. Unique. Show them loyalty only family could know and they'll give loyalty in return."

--

I hate sales funnels.

Or more specifically, I hate the idea of sales funnels and what they represent.

Let's think about it for a minute, funnels are straight, mechanical, boring. They're an automated way of pushing people to where you want them to go. It's all about driving to a conclusion, to the ultimate sale and getting the money in. It's an incredibly selfish way of looking at things, solely focused on the gain of the business, not the wants, needs and desires of the client. Now I'm not sure about you, but to me, that's not how I want to treat potential clients. I want them to be excited, to be motivated to progress, to look forward to the next part of their journey. The mind-numbing dullness of a sales funnel doesn't really quite capture that experience, does it?

I much prefer the idea of the "marble run". Similar in flow, as in you're taking someone from a start point to an end point, but that's where the similarities end.

A marble run is full of twists and turns, loops, gates, switches, wheels and pivots. A marble run is pure entertainment and enjoyment. A funnel most definitely isn't. If your potential clients were marbles (I know this is getting a bit meta, but stick with me…) and you wanted to show them the best time possible, would you choose to drop them in a funnel or a marble run?

Now some may argue that I'm just using different terms to describe the same thing - funnels, marble runs, at the end of the day, when built in reality they do pretty much the same thing and nurture potential clients through to a sale. And in reality, yes, the fundamentals don't differ, but the mindset and approach towards them does.

When you're thinking "funnels", you're thinking inward, about yourself, your own business and your own gain. When you're thinking "marble runs" however, the emphasis suddenly shifts outward, to the marble so to speak. You'll come at things from a completely different angle of "how can I make this the most enjoyable, creative and absorbing experience I can?".

That's the difference between the two. **It gets you out of the world of "selling" and into the world of "experience"**. Selling to someone doesn't make them buy. Nobody likes being sold to, right? But giving someone a unique, enjoyable and valuable experience will get them desperate to buy from you more than anything else.

The "Positive Pull"

So, we now know that a positive, memorable experience is a surefire way to get people wanting to work with (and pay) you more. And experience is all about emotion. How we feel.

The subject of emotions can be a deep and complex one, but for our purposes here, it's actually very simple. I call it the concept of **Positive Pull**.

We're constantly being pulled towards experiences that spark positive emotions in us. Likewise, we're always pushing ourselves away from experiences that cause negative emotions in us. The more positive emotions you can create and associate with your business, products, services and content, the more likely potential clients will stick around and want to deepen their relationships with you.

Our emotional states are the most powerful motivating factor we have. If we associate enough positivity with something, we'll do anything to achieve it. The same is true on the negative side. If we associate enough negativity with something, we'll do anything to get as far away as possible from it.

When we start thinking about the experiences that we offer and being more aware and strategic about the emotions we cause in people, we open up a very influential path to building trust.

There are **25 Emotional States**, both positive and negative:

Positive Emotional State	Description	Relative Negative Emotional State
Love	Feeling intimate and romantic towards someone	Hate
Admiration	Prize and esteem for someone for their worth/achievement	Apathy

Dreaminess	Calm state of introspection/thoughtfulness	Restlessness
Surprise	Pleased by something that happened suddenly/unexpectedly or unusual	Awareness
Energised	High-spirited state of being	Lethargic
Lust	Sexual appeal or appetite	Disgust
Attraction	Strong desire to enjoy or own something	Repulsion
Worship	Idolise, honour and be devoted to someone	Disdain
Courageous	Mental and moral strength to persevere and withstand danger or difficulty	Scared
Pride	Enjoyable sense of self-worth or achievement	Lowly
Confident	Faith in oneself or in one's abilities to achieve or act right	Doubtful
Sympathy	Identify with someone's feelings of misfortune or distress	Insensitive
Kindness	Protect or contribute to the wellbeing of someone	Cruel
Respectful	Regard someone as worthy, good or valuable	Rude
Euphoric	Carried away by an overwhelming sense of pure joy	Depressed
Happiness	Pleased about or taking pleasure in something or a desired event	Sadness
Amusement	Playful state of humour or entertainment	Boredom

Relief	Recent removal of stress or discomfort	Pained
Relaxed	Calm state of being, free from physical or mental tension or concern	Stressed
Satisfied	Recent fulfilment of a need or desire	Unfulfilled
Inspired	Sudden and overwhelming feeling of creative impulse	Unmotivated
Enchanted	Captivated by something delightful or extraordinary	Disinterested
Fascinated	Urge to explore, investigate or understand something	Indifferent
Hopeful	Belief that something good or wished for could possibly happen	Fearful
Anticipation	Eagerly await a desirable event that's expected to happen	Anxiety

People will usually come to us because they're experiencing some form of negative emotional state. There's a problem in their lives that's causing it and they want to sort out that problem so they can move from a state of negative emotion to positive emotion. It really is as simple as that. And **it's our job as business owners and service providers to give them the quickest, most effective way possible of reaching that positive state.**

The 5 Stages Of Awareness

We're always starting with a negative state to fix. That's essentially the whole purpose of our business. The client has a problem, we have the solution, the client moves into a positive state when we deliver the desired result.

But not all negative states are created equal, and we really need to consider this when talking with potential clients. Different people have different levels of awareness of the negative emotions that they feel. Some are fully aware of how they're feeling and why, some don't even know they have a problem.

In 1966, one of the modern masters of marketing, *Eugene Schwartz*, released the groundbreaking book *"Breakthrough Advertising"*. In it, he lays out the framework for the **5 Stages Of Awareness** - an incredibly helpful tool for determining which stage of awareness your potential clients are in, and more importantly, how you should be talking to them to move them to the next stages, ready to buy.

Stage #1: Unaware

At this stage, a person doesn't even know they have a problem, but are still experiencing the negative emotional effects without realising it.

When speaking to your potential clients who may be here, it's actually about connecting the dots between the negative emotional state they're in and the problem that's likely causing it.

For example, as I've done in this book, you're feeling the pain of stress in your business, but you may not have known exactly why. I've given you the problem of "lead-hustling" and the reasons as to why that's the cause. **I'm connecting the dots between the pain and the problem.**

Now people progress to the next stage…

Stage # 2: Problem Aware

At this stage, people realise they have a particular problem, but don't know of any solutions to make it better.

For potential clients that are here, they're feeling the negative emotional state and they now know why they're feeling it. They understand they have a problem. **Now it's your job to introduce them to the best option(s) open to them to sort out the problem they're facing.** Again, taking the example from this book, I introduced you to the problem of "lead-hustling" and then to remedy that, I've told you that you need to focus on acquiring paying customers only, and the benefits of doing so.

Stage #3: Solution Aware

At this stage, people know about the general solution(s) available to them but haven't chosen one yet. They also don't know about your particular solution (product or service).

Now that your potential clients know what the general solution is to their problem, it's time to introduce them to your specific solution. That's how you move them on to the next stage of being Product Aware.

In this book, I've taken you through the problem, I've outlined an overall solution and then I'm introducing you to the **Zero Leads** method - a specific framework that will solve the problem of "lead-hustling" and take away all the associated negative emotions you're currently feeling.

Stage #4: Product Aware

At this stage, people know about your solution but are still deciding if it's the best fit for them.

Once potential clients know about your product, it's your job to convince them that it's the best solution on the market to their problem. And there's a very easy way of doing this - by delivering value and results up front. By taking the very initial steps of your solution and giving it to them so they can see a positive impact in their business immediately.

Nothing says "I can help you" more than actually *helping* someone.

On top of giving them an instant initial result up front, they'll also be looking at a personality and value fit. 99% of the time, there'll be other options available to them that'll get them the result they're looking for (unless you have a patented product or process). But **just as important as the "what" you're delivering is the "how" you're delivering it**.

We'll be looking into this more in the next chapter, but for now, just know that the results you offer are only half the story, the other half is all down to that all-important "experience" we've already spoken about.

Stage #5: Most Aware

At this stage, people know everything about your solution and are very close to purchasing, they're just waiting for the right offer.

So now your potential client knows they want to work with you. They feel that after everything you've been through with them about your solution, it's the perfect fit. They're confident that you can deliver on your promises and turn their world of negative emotion into a positive state. The last piece of the puzzle is the offer.

Your offer is one of the most important things you have in your business. Get it right, and potential clients will be automatically drawn to working with you. Get it wrong however, and it can destroy all of the good work you've put in up until this point. In *Part 3* of this book, I'll be taking you through the exact steps to defining your irresistible **Signature Offers**. They're the main things you need to get right and are the first things you need to have done.

I hope you can now see that in order to move people from their negative states to acting on their desire to achieve a positive one, you need to take them through this process of awareness. **If you offer your services to someone that doesn't even realise they have a** problem, you won't convert them into a client, no matter how hard you try. The journey that you go on with your clients is crucial, and this is exactly what we're going to look into next.

The 6 Relationship Gates

Every potential client you have is not a sale waiting to be made, it's a relationship waiting to be built. Sales are made on solid relationships, not pitches. The stronger the relationship you can build with someone, the more likely they'll want to work with you. It's a very simple premise - **we work with and spend time with people we like.**

Think about all your best clients. You enjoy working with them because you like them. Time spent with them is fun and productive. It's relaxed and natural. You can have a laugh but get some seriously awesome work going on at the same time. They respect you and you respect them. You're both working together towards the same goal and it all just seems effortless. It's the same if you've worked for a company. You tend to form good working relationships with those you like. You tend to work more closely with those you like.

Business is just another word for relationships. The only difference to those in your personal life is that there's (usually) a monetary exchange of value. **The first and most important goal in business is to create valuable "win-win" relationships**. A balance where there's equal effort, respect and value. A great relationship is one where both parties profit. Where the lives and situations of both are made equally better because of the other.

There's usually an issue I find here though, and I've seen it time and time again. As soon as you put the word "business" in front of "relationship", a lot of people start losing their minds. Like building a relationship in business is something entirely different to building a personal, social relationship. Suddenly it becomes this weird, false, often smarmy attempt to "gain" the other's favour. A tiring display of "one-upmanship" and "peacocking", of firm handshake battles and loudest-voice-wins competitions.

Just to set the record straight now. **There's absolutely no difference in building a business relationship to that of a personal one.**

At the end of the day, we're all people. We all bond in the same way since the dawn of time. Forget that there's money involved, that doesn't matter and seems to cloud the issue with some people. Just focus on the individual in front of you and getting to know them. It really is as simple as that.

When we look to build new relationships with someone, there's a **6-stage process** called the **6 Relationship Gates** that we all go through (in business and out):

Gate #1: Attraction

The first stage is purely superficial. It's completely based on looks. I'm sure you've heard the statistic that in a job interview, the interviewer generally makes up their mind if they're going to hire the person in the first few milliseconds? That's a prime example of the subconscious mind at work.

Just to take a step back for a second, quite a while back actually to the dawn of humankind (bet you didn't see that coming…). As we were fighting for our survival from the dangers all around us, our brains developed the "fight-or-flight" connections that kept us safe. These connections had to be lightening quick, acting almost instantly to prevent us coming to any possible harm. They're completely subconscious and happen without us realising. They're based on senses, feelings, emotions and memories.

As we developed over the many thousands of years since then, our brains have developed further. On top of the "fight-or-flight" emotional system (more commonly known as the Limbic System), we've also fortunately grown the "rational logic" system (the Neo-Cortex). This system allows us to weigh up pro's and con's and to work out complex hypothetical situations. Basically, all the non-emotional stuff.

Now, while we might like to think of ourselves as highly rational creatures, the opposite in fact is true. Even though we're not literally fighting for our lives from the dangers of the natural world anymore, we still filter everything we experience through the emotional system in our brains first. Call it a force of habit I suppose.

We still have an instant, subconscious "gate" that needs to be crossed before our brains pass the information up to our Neo-Cortex for us to "think" about it.

Have you ever looked at something or someone and felt an immediate attraction? That you couldn't help but be enticed and wanted to know more? Your judgements weren't based on anything else except for what you could see. Purely visual. And from something so superficial, you had made the decision that, whatever it was, was right for you. Seems crazy, right? With no other information, just on looks alone.

Now, I'm not saying we base all our decisions on the way someone or something looks, that *would* be crazy. But, it's an incredibly important part in the first stages of relationship-building.

Where there's attraction, there's a much stronger desire to form a relationship. Without it you face an uphill battle to convince someone that you're worth their time.

In the next chapter, I'm going to take you through each of the areas you need to focus on to make sure that you're maximising your levels of attraction to your potential clients. We're going to look more deeply into your **brand**.

Gate #2: Curiosity

Once you've succeeded in the initial attraction on an emotional level, we then need to appeal to the rational part of the brain.

The best way to do this is to give it something unusual and mysterious to chew on. It needs to be novel and it needs to keep people guessing. When you're attracted to someone or something, it suddenly becomes a fun and desirable game to know more. It's an adventure to tie up all of the loose ends going through your head about who they are, what they know, how they can enhance your life, how you can enhance theirs etc. And it all starts with a **hook**.

The best hooks are short, promise a massive benefit, but don't go into the answer. They merely tease them. As much as I can't stand clickbait, this is one area where curiosity is key. Yes, it's used in the wrong way here, more for trickery and financial gain rather than building an honest, profitable relationship with someone, but the headlines are perfected to deliver on the curiosity angle.

Even though I understand the nature and purpose of them. Even though I dislike and distrust them. I *still* find myself clicking on them sometimes because my curiosity got the better of me. And that's exactly where the best curiosity pulls come from - **headlines**.

Headlines can be an ad headline, a landing page title, an email subject line etc. Anything that sparks the desire in someone to know more. In fact, your headlines will be your most read pieces of content in your business. Get them right, and people will read on further. Get them wrong however, and the headline could be the only thing they ever read!

Curiosity is the key to deepening a relationship with someone. It's another form of attraction, but instead of on an emotional level, it acts on a rational level to complete the two.

Gate #3: Interest

The next stage is all about payoff.

You've attracted them with the way you've presented yourself, you've built curiosity and enticed them with novel hooks that promise to improve their lives somehow, now it's time to deliver on that curiosity. It's time to delve deeper and answer all the questions they have in their heads.

In a business context, this is where you go fully into the benefits you can offer them. The positive changes and impact you can make to their lives. You want to flesh out the "better future" they're looking for and go into every little detail. Make it real to them. Show them how you fit into the picture of helping them get there.

Better yet, show them how you've already made the lives of others like them better. Show them the real-world results that you've helped achieve for people. This will make your claims hard to ignore.

There's nothing that interests us more than ourselves. If you can focus on them and improving their situation, they'll reward you with tons of interest and engagement.

You'll then want to go into more about you, your business, your products and your services. This is where you go into the results you deliver and the frameworks you use to make them happen. Show them your processes, show them your skills and expertise.

You ultimately want to give them every piece of information they could want to help them make an informed decision on deepening the relationship further with you.

Gate #4: Enlightenment

Talking about results is great, it's definitely a very effective way of moving a new relationship forward with a potential client. But delivering results is even better. Getting someone to experience first-hand that "this could actually work for me", is a game-changer.

Have you ever been on a date with someone that's enthusiastically telling you about all the great things they do in their lives whilst they sip their glass of wine? You're thinking in your head "Wow, this person is so interesting! If I spend more time with them, my life will become more interesting also!".

But then as you start spending more time with them, you begin to realise that their words were hollow. They don't actually do any of that stuff and were just trying to impress you. They'd done a great job at the first 3 stages, they attracted you, both emotionally and rationally with their appearance and curiosity. They piqued your interest with their "insight" into their lives and how they could potentially benefit yours. But they failed on delivering.

This is where the Enlightenment stage is so crucially important and is the stage that most people and businesses screw up on.

In order to convince people that you can make their lives better, you need to actually make their lives better.

You need to prove this to them *before* they've committed fully to you.

There's one very simple way of doing this - delivering results upfront. Think about their ideal future, where they want to be, their desires, and give them the first step of that journey. What's the first thing they need or need to do to set them up for success and the future they want? Show them that it's possible. Show them you can deliver on your promises by actually delivering on your promises.

It doesn't need to be massive, but it needs to be valuable. It needs to be something that kickstarts the momentum and can change their beliefs about what's possible for them because of your help and support.

Belief is a huge part of enlightenment and we'll be looking at belief in more depth later in this book.

Gate #5: Commitment

This is the holy grail of all relationships. When there's commitment, from both sides, there's the potential for greatness. When there's equal commitment, there's value and benefit for both parties.

Commitment is essentially the decision to enter into a trusting, profitable value exchange. The length of that commitment depends on the commitment itself, but the terms are always the same. It must be win-win. **If there's imbalance and one side is benefiting more than the other, it's not a relationship, it's exploitation.**

I want to just break out from this point here, as I think this is something that's very important and worth highlighting.

I see so many freelancers struggle in this area and unfortunately spend the majority of their working lives being exploited. **There's immense value in what you do and what you can bring to the lives of others. It's only fair that you are accurately compensated for that value.**

Too many freelancers devalue their work and value by undercharging. Their clients get a great deal - profitable results for practically nothing. However, the service provider gets stress and the potential to "just about cover the bills". That's definitely not the sign of a good relationship. A good relationship is based on respect and equality, of fair value exchange.

We'll be looking at pricing in *Chapter 10*, but I want you to know this. I created the **Zero Leads** method for the freelancers out there that are stuck in exploitative client relationships. That want out of working for those that take advantage of them, that don't respect and value their skills and abilities, that don't offer up an equal value exchange.

The **Zero Leads** method is a way of gaining control back. It's a way to bypass those shitty clients and start attracting clients that want to commit to a prosperous relationship with you.

It's ultimately about creating products, services and offers that help build the right kind of relationships with your ideal clients, so you can not only start enjoying what you do again, but also get paid your worth for doing it.

Gate #6: Integration

The final step in any new relationship is integration. This is when you're confident in your choices and decisions, you trust in the other person, and now you want to expand outside of the world of just the "two" of you. It's when you introduce your newfound relationship to the rest of your world - your friends, your family, your colleagues etc.

Integration is about fitting the new relationship into the rest of your life and the lives of others you know by sharing it and shouting about it. It's that "meet the parents" kind of time…

In business, that's when a client starts introducing you to others they know. Others like them that could use your help. Essentially, **referrals**.

There are **2 types of referral** you can get from a client:

- **Direct referral**

    This is what's known as "word-of-mouth", the most powerful sales tactic of all! If you can build an "army" of happy, loyal clients that spread the word about you to their friends and fellow business associates, you'll have the most potent sales force you could ever hope for. And the beauty of it? It's free.

    They refer because they love working with you, because they trust in your ability to deliver, and more importantly, because it makes them look good!

    Think about it, if you find something that's awesome, that only you know about, and you start telling others about it, they'll associate the "awesomeness" of that something with you, because you recommended it to them. It's kind of like piggybacking on the positive good of others, but in a nice way.

    We want to be the ones with the "next-best-secret". We want to be the ones that can help where no-one else can. We want to be the ones that people start coming to for advice and be seen as the expert in a certain area - it's why we do what we do, right?

And it's this desire in all of us that compels us to tell others when we've found a good thing - and that's very good news for you!

- **Indirect referral**

    Indirect referrals are basically quotes, testimonials and case studies. They're not directly transferred from the client to someone they know, but are instead collected by you to give out to your potential clients as social proof of your ability to deliver results.

    The **Zero Leads** method has indirect referral gathering baked into it, as it's such an important part of your ability to grow and scale your business.

    We'll be looking into exactly how you can automatically gather social proof from your clients in *Chapter 8*.

Bringing It All Together

So, we've looked at the **6 Relationship Gates**, the concept of **Positive Pull**, the **25 Emotional States** and the **5 Stages Of Awareness**. That's quite a lot to go through I admit, and you're probably wondering how they all fit together, so let's do just that.

To give a quick recap, clients go through a relationship-building process with you. As they go through that process, they also increase their levels of awareness about their own problems, the solutions available to them and your ability to help them.

That's the factual side of things. There's also the emotional side of things to think about. As they go through the new relationship process, they're also feeling certain things, and it's our job as service providers to transform those feelings from negative to positive at each step, so we can move the relationship forward.

Here's how it all comes together:

Relationship Gates	Stages Of Awareness	Undesirable Negative States	Desirable Positive States
-	Unaware		
Attraction	Problem Aware	Repulsion	Attracted
Curiosity		Indifferent, aware	Fascinated, surprised
Interest	Solution / Product Aware	Unmotivated, bored, fearful	Inspired, amused, hopeful
Enlightenment	Most Aware	Anxious, lethargic, scared, doubtful	Anticipation, energised, courageous, confident
Commitment		Pained, unfulfilled, sadness, apathy	Relief, satisfaction, happiness, admiration
Integration		Lowliness, disdain	Pride, worship

This is how we build relationships with potential clients through the **Zero Leads** method. This is what will create massive profitability in your business. If you take people step-by-step through this process and foster those desirable positive states (which the **Zero Leads** method is specifically built to do), then you'll see radical shifts in the amount of success you experience.

I've spent quite a bit of time going through this, because it's crucial to your success with this system. As much as the tactics of the **Zero Leads** method are important, the theory and philosophy behind them are even more so.

Once you understand the deeper objectives that we're trying to achieve with this system, you'll have a much clearer idea as to why every part of the **Zero Leads** framework is set up like it is.

It's easy to just copy something and implement it, but unless you know the "why" behind it all, you won't be able to fully own and expand on it in your business.

Key Takeaways:

- Stop thinking about "sales funnels" and start thinking about "marble runs". Place a client-first approach into your sales process and start delivering value, enjoyment and entertainment. Your goal is not to make a sale, it's to make a relationship. **Sales are just the natural conclusion to a successful business relationship.**

- We're all pulled towards things that make us happy and put us into positive states of emotion. In order to successfully build relationships with potential clients we need to constantly be moving them from any negative states they may be feeling to positive ones. By doing so we build trust and a desire to deepen the relationship. **Whenever you're dealing with a potential client, think about how they're feeling and how you can make them feel even better!**

- All new client relationships go through different stages of growth and awareness. We have to satisfy both the emotional side (the Limbic System) and the rational side (the Neo-Cortex) of the brain in order to move the relationship forward. Depending on which stage you're currently at with a potential client, you'll need to change the way you speak to them and what you speak to them about to move them along their journey. You want to get them from knowing nothing about their problem or your business as a possible solution, to a highly valuable, paying client that refers your services to everyone they know.

7
HOW TO CONSISTENTLY ATTRACT 5-FIGURE CLIENTS...FOR FREE

"We talk about engaging with others. But fail to engage with ourselves. How can we connect externally when we neglect the internal? Dismiss our own needs and desires. Our own thoughts and feelings. We fall in line. Play to expectations. Even though they may not be our own. But how would we know? Unless we listen to us. Talk to us. Engage with us. To engage with others, they need to know who they're engaging with. How would they know if we don't? Find out who you are first. Take that person to others. That's when true engagement begins."

--

Attracting your ideal clients thankfully isn't as difficult as some make it out to be.

It's simply a combination of creativity and economics.

In this chapter, we're going to look into both. First, we'll focus on the creative side, and then we'll back it up with the economic foundation. Don't worry, it's a very simple concept, but once you know it, it'll be very hard to look at anything in your business quite the same again!

We know that attraction is the first stage in any new relationship. We also know that attraction is mainly the area of the Limbic (emotional) system in our brains. There are **5 Connective Qualities** that we generally (and subconsciously) go through in order when we're attracted to someone. These are where you really need to be on the top of your game when meeting new potential clients:

The 5 Connective Qualities

Quality #1: Perceptive Connection

99% of the time, the first impression of others (people and businesses) that we have is visual. It's the exact reason why phrases like "don't judge a book by its cover" exist. We're urged to look deeper, beyond the surface to make a truly informed decision about something or someone. And the reason we have to be *urged* is because our natural tendency is to make snap decisions based on appearances.

That's why it's crucial to present yourself in the best light possible. To make sure that you're maximising your opportunity to connect with your potential clients' "fight-or-flight" instincts. **You need to make sure that as soon as they see your business, it screams quality and trustworthiness.** It needs to pass that first few "milliseconds test", for them to even consider wanting to learn more about you and what you have to offer.

And the way you do that?

Your visual identity.

Or what's more commonly referred to as, the "way you look".

There are a number of key elements that you'll need to purposefully think about in your business including:

- The colours you use

- The shapes you use

- The fonts you use

- The images you use

- The icons you use

- The layout you use

Each of these areas have a different psychological impact depending on what choices you make. But therein lies the rub. In the majority of cases, business owners make the wrong choices. Usually because they don't understand the psychological aspects of the choices they make. In fact, the main reason why business owners get it wrong is this:

They choose based on *their* likes, not the likes of their *audience*.

Every design choice you make needs to have a distinct reason. And the reason should be attracting and connecting with your ideal clients more. Every choice needs to amplify a positive perception of you and your business.

Quality #2: Character Connection

When you've succeeded with the initial attraction, you'll need to deepen the connection by introducing them more to your personality. The worst thing you can do at this point is be caught in the "beauty's only skin deep" frame, so make sure you have substance to back up your look.

Your personality isn't about *what* you communicate, but *how* you communicate. It must be consistent with your visual identity. If the way you look gives the feeling of calmness and relaxation, you'll instantly turn people off if your personality is loud, energetic and "in-your-face".

Your potential clients will want and expect a certain type of personality as they look to deepen their relationship with you. Again, some people will love your personality, others won't. And that's fine. Don't alter your personality to please everyone. That's the fastest route to bland, generic and boring. Be passionate. Bring "you" to the table. **Your friends love you for a reason, show your potential clients that reason also.**

It's not a very complicated point, so don't overthink it. You are the figurehead of your business, so your business personality will come from you. Just make sure it's the best parts of *you* you're showing!

There are **3 main ways** that potential clients will be introduced to your personality:

1. Through your written content

2. Through your video/audio content

3. Through calls with you (and your team)

When it's just you working in your business it's easy to maintain your personality. But as you expand and grow your team in line with your increasing number of clients, you'll need to make sure your personality is known, understood and carried out by each one of them. That's why if you can document your personality traits from the beginning, it'll be easier to grow and maintain it rather than losing it in the growth process.

Quality #3: Ethical Connection

We're starting to get a little deeper now. They like the look of you, they like your personality. Now they want to know what you stand for. Do you share the same values and beliefs? Do you have similar ideals that you live by?

If you think about all the social friends you have, you'll notice that you share certain values with them. You connect on a deeper level.

Shared values are crucial to building trusting connections and relationships. We see it in life the world over. Groups and cultures form and come together over communal beliefs. It's no different in business. You'll naturally have competitors in your niche that provide similar products and services to you, but what can make you stand out from the rest are your unique values.

Think about what you value most in business and life. Then find out what your ideal clients value the most in these areas. Where there's overlap, shout about it!

We'll always look to work with those that we share values with. Because they're like us. We understand them. We can *trust* them.

Those we don't won't get a look in.

Quality #4: Relative Connection

To deepen the connection further, we need to go beyond shared values and look to shared experiences. When we know that we're interacting with someone that not only understands us, but has also been through similar things to us, we become infinitely more open to trusting them.

This is where it's so important to share your story.

Your story is about your journey of success. The same success that you're offering to your potential clients. All great stories follow this framework:

1. What was your life like before you found success?

2. What was the key moment in your life when you decided to change?

3. What were the main things at stake if you didn't succeed?

4. What initial things did you try to achieve your success?

5. What were the barriers and obstacles you came up against?

6. Where, what or who did you learn the "magic formula" from?

7. What exactly was the "magic formula"?

8. What happened in your business and life when you started using the "magic formula"?

9. How did your world change physically?

10. How did you change as a person mentally and emotionally?

When we tell stories, we're aiming to connect on a deeper, emotional level with people. Stories have been used for hundreds of thousands of years to pass knowledge, wisdom and experience to others.

Stories are the most effective method of forming empathy.

This story structure has been specifically created to seamlessly take people on a journey of discovery and understanding about you - and themselves. Your story is powerful because the beginning of it should mirror their story. Not in every detail, but in overall theme and direction. The beginning of your story empathises with where they are now. The current pains and challenges they have. The rest of your story offers them a way out. It gives them hope and belief that there's a way to change their exact circumstances, and you're the best person to help them.

ructure is based on *The Hero's Journey* by *Joseph Campbell* and has ...ed countless times over in top Hollywood films and best-selling fiction books. It's popular because it *works*. Because it's the best way to hook people in and keep them hanging on until the end.

This is another area that I see a lot of businesses fail on. They focus too much on their products and services, but not on their story. Did you know that the "about" page on websites is usually the second most visited page after the homepage? Why? Because people want to know who you are and what you're about. And your story is how you tell them.

Quality #5: Momentum Connection

Finally, we usually want to develop relationships with people that inspire us. That are constantly working towards something and never standing still. They have an overarching agenda of improvement and betterment. They have a new vision of the world that they're trying to make happen. They have a mission that they're on and goals to achieve it. They have a cause that they're fighting for. These are the people that inspire us, and these are the people we follow and listen to. Their passion is infectious. We want to surround ourselves with people that can make a difference, to themselves, to us, and to the world around us in some way.

I want you to think about your vision for a better world. How would you want a better world to look? Something that you could make a difference towards? What mission are you on? How can you improve the lives and situations of others?

Ultimately, how can you leave this world a better place than you found it?

How would you want to leave this world for your children?

When you passionately follow a path, people will follow you. It doesn't matter what path it is, just make it your path. Your path is born from your own life experiences. It's unique to you. You can't follow the paths of others, it won't be genuine and people will realise that from a mile off. It needs to be true to your beliefs. True to your values and true to your heart.

That's how tribes form. That's how movements are made.

I see a lot of business owners neglecting everything we've gone through in this chapter so far. They see it as unnecessary. Of not directly getting to the sale. Almost a "waste of time" in some cases. But these **5 Connective Qualities** are the foundation of every good relationship.

The 7 Connection Maximisers

I also want to introduce you to the **7 Connection Maximisers**. If the *Qualities* are the fertile soil, then the *Maximisers* are the water. Pour these on to any relationship and watch it grow stronger and faster:

Maximiser #1: Communication

First up is the #1 key (or killer) of any relationship. Communication is critical. The better we communicate, the better our relationships. It really is as simple as that. Good communication is based on being regular, clear, simple, transparent and timely.

Maximiser #2: Respect

For any relationship to grow, there must be a mutual level of respect for one another. That's respect for each other's thoughts, feelings, skills & abilities, choices, lifestyle, desires, ideals, values and boundaries. We're all equal and we all bring something different to the table. It doesn't matter if you're a hardcore veteran and been at it for years or you're just starting your journey. Without mutual respect, relationships quickly break down and become toxic.

Maximiser #3: Trust

To gain one another's trust, there must be a shared standard of values and goals. That you're both heading in the same direction. There has to be an equal balance of authenticity, honesty and commitment to the cause and to each other.

Trust is an enabler. When there's more trust, you can achieve greater results, faster and at lower cost. There's no wasted time. When trust is low, it takes much longer to get anywhere, the results will be of lower quality and it will ultimately cost more to get there.

Maximiser #4: Support

No-one has the ability or mental strength to take everything on in life by themselves. We all need support at some point. The old saying "two heads are better than one" ring true. Sometimes we all need somebody to lean on (thanks Bill Withers).

Support comes in many forms. Again, there must be an even balance of helping one another, guiding each other on our journeys in life, giving that "kick up the ass" motivation we all need once in a while, and most importantly, celebrating each other when we're striving to be the best we can be.

Maximiser #5: Entertainment

Remember we're always looking to move away from negative states towards positive states. It goes without saying then that fun and entertainment are high on the list when building and maintaining healthy, profitable relationships. It comes from a philosophy of making "play" deliberate. Of basing your interactions on humour and lightheartedness. Business is no different to social relationships. **You still need to be friends first.**

Maximiser #6: Interest

Now this isn't about *you* being interesting (which a lot of people mistake this point for). It's actually about you having an interest in the other person. Of understanding them and their situation. Of empathising with their successes and their failures. If you take it upon yourself to become an expert on them, they'll reward you with more trust than you can imagine.

Maximiser #7: Generosity

And lastly, we come to the very act of "delivering value up front". It's about going that extra mile for someone. Offering before you ask. But you have to be careful with this one.

As we've already spoken about, where there's already trust and respect, generosity will deepen the relationship further, but where there's none, you get imbalance. You get freeloaders leeching off your generosity without any desire to even the score.

We live in a funny world where generosity is used more as an incentive to start a new relationship than it is to strengthen existing relationships. Look at insurance quotes or bank accounts. New customers always get the best deals and rates to hook them in, but as soon as you're a loyal customer, you get ripped off with above average rates. Hardly a great way to build a strong, long-standing, profitable relationship with someone, right?

Generosity is a very powerful tool. Just make sure you're using it with the right people.

Get the **5 Connective Qualities** and the **7 Connection Maximisers** right and you'll be attracting your ideal clients all day long. You'll give yourself the very best chance of attracting them in the first place and maximising the potential that they'll become paying customers.
Those 2 concepts right there will massively offset your cost of acquiring them in the first place!

But that's not where it ends. Ultimately, we want our new customers for free, right? We're going to step away from the more intangible side of winning new clients to the 100% tangible. Great businesses have an equal balance of both, and that's where this simple but powerful little equation comes in to play...

The Free Client Formula

This is what I call the **Free Client Formula**, and it looks like this:

> **CPA < AOV = Guaranteed Profitable Growth**

Let's just take a minute to break this down into each individual part:

CPA

This stands for **Cost Per Acquisition.**

Whenever you acquire a client, there's always a cost associated with it. It doesn't matter if you've directly paid to acquire them (paid advertising), or indirectly paid to acquire them (your time, or outsource costs for content creation and marketing activity).

In order to grow your business, you must know this number.

There's a very simple formula for this also:

> **(Content Creation Costs + Paid Ad Costs) / No. Of New Acquisitions = CPA**

It's easy to figure out your **Paid Ad Costs**, it'll just be the total budget that you've spent with Facebook, Google etc.

Your **Content Creation Costs** are a little trickier, but not that difficult.

It'll either be the combination of fixed amount payments you made to a number of contractors (designers, copywriters etc.), or it'll be the number of hours you've worked creating everything, multiplied by your hourly rate.

Now, when I'm talking about hourly rate, I'm not talking about a client-facing charge. I would recommend staying away from hourly-rate pricing in your business. What I'm actually referring to is your hourly opportunity cost (i.e. the amount you could've earned working in the most profitable area of your business for that hour).

Most people are aware of their **Paid Ad Costs**, but few business owners take into account their **Content Creation Costs**, especially if they're creating everything themselves. But they're still equally as important to include. Let's go into a quick example just so everything's clear:

In this example, our mate Ben ran a Facebook ad campaign for one month. The total ad spend for that month was $1,000. Ben also spent 4 days creating everything and setting the ads up (so let's call that 20 hours in total). Ben usually earns $200 per hour when working with his clients. The result of the ad campaign was 500 new client acquisitions.

Let's lay this out another way:

Content Creation Cost	Paid Ad Cost	No. Of New Acquisitions	Cost Per Acquisition
$4,000	$1,000	500	$10
(20 hours x $200 rate)			($5,000 total cost / 500)

Is that making sense?

You need to take into account all of your costs per acquisition. Only then do you know what you need to make to balance them out.

Now, if you're just starting out in your business, or you aren't full of clients yet, then you'll probably have more free time than money. In that case, you'll have to do the content creation yourself, so the "cost" isn't something tangible.

But if you do have a lot of clients, and you can quite easily fill your hours with project work and earn $200 per hour from it, then you absolutely need to know this cost so you can make a decision...

Do you do it yourself? Or do you get someone else to do it?

Ben knows that he could earn $4,000 in client work over those 4 days it would take him to create all the content for the ad campaign. But he also knows a great graphic designer, copywriter and ads manager that could get everything together and running for him for $3,000. And they could do it in 2 days.

Suddenly it makes financial sense to outsource the entire job, doesn't it? Not only does it get done in half the time, but Ben also has an extra $1,000 kept in the business. He used those 4 days to earn $4,000 and he's only spent $3,000, instead of losing 4 days ($4,000) of client work while he worked on it himself.

This isn't something that's strictly necessary to grasp the idea of **Cost Per Acquisition**, but nonetheless it's an incredibly important point that so many business owners fail to take into account. I don't want you to be one of those business owners. I want you to be in full control of your finances and the options available to you.

To take it back to the basic idea, just remember that you need to add your **Paid Ad Costs** to your **Content Creation Costs** and divide that total by the number of acquisitions you get, to get your **CPA**.

AOV

This stands for **Average Order Value**.

It's basically the average amount of revenue you receive from every newly acquired customer. Or, "what they pay you when they first sign up". There really isn't that much to it. To calculate this, just use the following:

Total Order Revenue / No. Of New Acquisitions = AOV

If we go back to our mate Ben, we know that he managed to bring in 500 new acquisitions from his Facebook ad campaign. Each one of those new customers spent $5. Therefore, his **Total Order Revenue** was $2,500. We don't need to go back and do the **AOV** formula in this instance because we already know that each new acquisition spent $5. So, the **AOV** is $5.

Total Order Revenue	No. Of New Acquisitions	Average Order Value
$2,500	500	$5
($5 x 500 people)		

So now that we have both the **CPA** and the **AOV**, we can go back to the **Free Client Formula** and plug in the numbers:

CPA	AOV	Guaranteed Profitable Growth?
$10	$5	No
(If Ben did everything himself)		(CPA is not less than AOV)

We can see that for this particular campaign, Ben lost money (sorry Ben). The revenue he bought in from new acquisition orders did not cover all his costs.

Ben now has two options to try and fix this. He either:

1. Tries to *reduce* his **CPA**, or…

2. Tries to *increase* his **AOV**.

Let's look at each of these options more closely:

Reducing Your CPA

When you're experiencing high **CPA's**, there are a few things you can do about this:

- Outsource to others that can do it cheaper and quicker than you (as we've already looked at).

- Change your ad creative (image, headline, body copy, offer, landing page design etc.).

- Change who you're targeting your ad at (you might just be showing the right thing to the wrong people).

I won't go into detail about these points in this book. There's literally a whole separate book I could write on the subject of ad optimisation - and that's not what this book is about. But I wanted to give you an overview of your options, so you know where to start looking.

Once you have these all in check however, there are only marginal gains you can make with your **CPA**. You'll soon come to a point where you've hit close to your optimum. Anything beyond that will be looking at small percentage points, not massive reductions in cost.

When you reach that point, the only way you're going to start winning in the **Free Client Formula** is to look at increasing your **AOV**.

Increasing Your AOV

Now here's where things get really interesting. Because here you're in full control and the sky really is the limit. It just depends on how well you implement what we'll be talking about over the next few pages.

Let's say Ben's optimal **CPA** is at that $10 mark we figured out earlier. He knows that he needs to increase his **AOV** to at least match that (and preferably be more than it).

This is where "order bumps" and "upsells" come into play.

Previously, Ben only offered a $5 product to sign new customers up to his list. A nice small amount with a low barrier to entry. A price someone wouldn't even think twice about if they were remotely interested in what Ben was offering.

But the problem is, it's not enough.

Now, what would happen if Ben added a $30 product as an order bump? We can safely assume that not everyone would opt to add this to their order, but what if 30% of new acquisitions did? Let's look at the math.

First, we need to work out the **Total Order Revenue**:

> **Initial Order Revenue + Order Bump Revenue = Total Order Revenue**

Initial Order Revenue	Order Bump Revenue	Total Order Revenue
$2,500	$4,500	$7,000
($5 x 500 people)	($30 x (500 x 0.3))	($2,500 + $4,500)

That's looking a little healthier now!

Let's plug that back into the **Free Client Formula** and see where Ben stands now.

CPA	AOV	Guaranteed Profitable Growth?
$10	$14	Yes
(If Ben did everything himself)	($7,000 / 500 people)	(CPA is slightly less than AOV)

That single, simple addition has now made a world of difference. It's completely shifted Ben's campaign from making a $5 loss per new acquisition to a $4 gain! All from adding one $30 order bump to the initial sign-up offer.

So, Ben's campaign is now driving a profit for him even before he's mentioned his premium services. It's bringing him in new customers and he's the one being paid for doing so!

But why stop there?

What about upsells?

Whereas order bumps are smaller amounts, generally in the $10-50 range, upsells are usually around the $100-300 range, and beyond in some cases. I've actually seen initial upsells in the thousands, but they're few and far between and I wouldn't recommend it for 99% of businesses.

Naturally, as we move up the price ranges, less and less of your initial acquisitions will take you up on the offers. So, let's see how the math adds up.

Ben is pretty happy with his **AOV** of $14, but knows he can do better and also offer better value to those new acquisitions that want it. He decides to add two upsells to his initial offer. One at $100. The other at $300. 10% take him up on his $100 upsell offer and 2% take him up on his $300 offer.

Here's how the figures look with the upsells added in:

Initial Order Revenue	Order Bump Revenue (at 30%)	Upsell 1 Revenue (at 10%)	Upsell 2 Revenue (at 2%)	Total Order Revenue
$2,500	$4,500	$5,000	$3,000	$15,000
($5 x 500 people)	($30 x (500 x 0.3)	($100 x (500 x 0.1)	($300 x (500 x 0.02)	

Even with those much smaller percentages of new acquisitions buying the upsells, again, the difference in **Total Order Revenue** is massive! For the final time, let's put these figures back into the **Free Client Formula**:

CPA	AOV	Guaranteed Profitable Growth?
$10	$30	Yes!
(If Ben did everything himself)	($15,000 / 500 people)	(CPA is much less than AOV)

That's the power of order bumps and upsells. They've transformed Ben's results from losing $5 on every new customer to making a profit of $20 on each of them!

If that's what happens with $1,000 ad spend in a month, what happens when Ben spends $2,000? $10,000? $100,000 even?

The **Free Client Formula** unlocks your ability to scale your ad spend as much as you want, because you always know you'll be instantly making that money back...and more. That's the key to rapid growth. And it's the point when you can use the profits from the very beginning to grow a team of people to help and do it for you. Designers, copywriters, ad managers, sales staff, VAs etc. All because you put a system in place that allows you to do so.

And when you come to the point that your **CPA** starts to rise (which you definitely will due to ad fatigue etc.), you simply switch that campaign off, create a new one and start it all over again.

That's how you get new clients for free (or even better, get paid to get new clients). And this is the fundamental premise that the **Zero Leads** method is based on. A premise that doesn't rely on any particular platform or creative. It's a premise that's universal and stands the test of time - because it's simple economics.

Seeing as we're on the subject of hard figures, there's one more incredibly important figure I want to introduce you to, just to round off the main trio.

The **AOV** is perfect when you're looking at offsetting your acquisition costs, but when you want to look at your overall potential profitability, you'll need to know your **ALTV**.

ALTV

This stands for **Average Life Time Value.**

It's incredibly similar to **AOV**, but instead focuses on the entire revenue you get from all of your clients including your premium service offers.

The basic formula looks like this:

> **(Acquisition Order Revenue + Premium Service Revenue) / Total No. Of Clients = ALTV**

Going back to Ben then, we know that for every 500 new clients he brings in, he makes $15,000 in revenue from the **Acquisition Orders**. Ben also offers a $5,000 coaching program and a $50,000 "done-for-you" service. 2% of people join the coaching program and 0.5% of people go for the premium "done-for-you" service.

When we lay this out, the figures look like this:

Acquisition Order Revenue	Coaching Revenue (at 2%)	"Done-For-You" Revenue (at 0.5%)	Average Life Time Value
$15,000	$50,000	$100,000*	$330
	($5,000 x (500 x 0.02)	($50,000 x (500 x 0.005)	($165,000 / 500)

*A quick point here that 0.5% of 500 people is 2.5, which would come out as $125,000 in "done-for-you" revenue. Unfortunately though, try as we might, we can't split people in half for more revenue, so we have to round down to 2 "full" people that take up the service. Therefore $100,000 in revenue.

As you can see, when we start looking at **ALTV**, we get a real understanding of the profitability of our business. A brand-new client is worth on average $30 to Ben. However, each client will ultimately spend on average $330 with Ben.

Just to summarise then, that initial $5,000 ad campaign cost has resulted in 500 new clients and $165,000 in revenue. That's some serious return! And that's why the **Zero Leads** method is so powerful!

But I'm sure you're thinking "well if it's that easy, why isn't everyone doing it?", and you'd be right. The maths of it are simple and concrete. The implementation of it is a lot more complex. Luckily enough, in the next chapter, I'm going to take you through the exact step-by-step process of achieving it and everything you'll need along the way.

In the next chapter, we're doing a deep dive into the whole **Zero Leads** process.

Key Takeaways:

- In order to get new clients in, you'll need to attract them. Use the **5 Connective Qualities** to help speed up the journey of connection with your potential clients. Focus on purposefully designing and conveying your **Perception, Character, Ethical, Relative** and **Momentum Connection** traits. Your ideal clients won't be able to help but want to find out more.

- To deepen profitable relationships further, take advantage of the **7 Connection Maximisers** –

Communication, Respect, Trust, Support, Entertainment, Interest and **Generosity**. All great relationships are based on these. The more you have in yours, the more you'll get out of them.

- Knowing how to attract new clients is one thing, knowing how to attract them for free is another entirely. That's where the **Free Client Formula** comes in. **CPA < AOV = Guaranteed Profitable Growth.** It's as simple as that. As long as the cost you have for acquiring new clients is less than the initial revenue coming in, your business will grow. "Order bumps" and "upsells" are the perfect way to achieve this and are a key element of the **Zero Leads** method.

- Your true measure of profitability comes from your **Average Life Time Value (ALTV)**. This figure will give you the overall value of each client in your business. You can then use this figure to determine your cost and profit levels. The formula looks like this: **(Acquisition Order Revenue + Premium Service Revenue) / Total No. Of Clients = ALTV.**

8
HOW TO GO FROM "JUST MET" TO $50,000 PROJECT

"Your time is finite. There are only a set amount of hours in a day. Days in a year. Years in your life. There is a ceiling. A limit to where your own time can get you. Grow beyond your own time. Time is not the measure of your worth. Define your value by the value that you can offer the world. Systemise that value. Automate that value. Build that value so that you can one day step out of it. So that you can step back from the doing and start seeing. Start seeing the value grow at a rate far beyond your time. That is the true secret of growth."

--

For a client to choose to work with you, it's a matter of one thing and one thing only…

Belief.

In 99% of cases where something isn't quite working, businesses don't have a service problem, or a marketing problem, they have a *belief* problem.

Your job, as an expert in your field, is to change people's beliefs.

When we don't have belief, we pull back. We hesitate. We keep asking more questions, gathering more "proof". But belief is a game-changer. When we believe, we act. We jump into the unknown, head-first into new opportunities. We believe that there's a better option for us, and we'll do whatever it takes to make it happen.

That's the difference between amateurs and professionals. Amateurs only look to "sell". They're waiting to "tell" people what they need. To wax lyrical about what they have to offer and nothing more. They're there to convince and persuade. To force their way of thinking upon you.

Professionals however know that no matter how much you talk *at* someone, you'll never "make" them do anything. People don't do things because someone else said so, they do things because they believe it's the right thing for them to do. And in order to make people believe, you need to *lead* their minds to the answers, not force the answers upon them.

There are 3 stages of belief that you'll need to work through with every potential client, known as **The Belief Continuum**.

The Belief Continuum

Belief In The Result

The first belief that you'll need to change is in the possibility of a better option. A better way. A better life. You need to introduce them to a realistic solution to their current pains and challenges. It could be the case of opening their eyes to what that better life would look like, the method by which they achieve it, or both. Once they believe there's a better path for them, one that has already worked for others like them, they're ready to move onto the next stage.

Belief In You

Now that they believe in the result, you need to get them to believe that you, above all others, are the right person to help them achieve it. There are a few key elements here and they're all to do with character and experience.

First, they need to be able to put their trust in you. That you're honest, passionate, dedicated, empathetic, knowledgeable and balanced. You need to show them that they can fully depend on you to get them the result they desire. That you won't abuse their trust. Second, you need to let them into your story. Your experience. How has it mirrored their own? Why do you understand the pains and challenges they face? They need to know that you "get" them.

Belief In Themselves

Finally in **The Belief Continuum**, comes their own belief in themselves. It doesn't matter if they're completely sold on the result, are fully bought into you as a person and the only guide they need, if they don't believe that *they* can do it or achieve it, then they won't progress.

This is probably the most neglected part of all 3 stages. It's about overcoming the internal fears and negative associations we have. It's about shifting peoples' perspectives that are holding them back. This is the final key to unlocking progress. When you have belief in yourself, you can achieve anything.

When we look at **The Belief Continuum** in a practical and real-world context, most businesses are ok at the first stage (although a lot only talk about their products and services, not about the "better life" they offer). Fewer businesses fully go into their stories and empathise with their potential clients on a deeper level. And on the very rare occasion do businesses "coach" their potential clients' mindsets. To help them overcome their own internal battles and barriers that are stopping them from achieving the success they seek.

I wanted to give you a brief overview of that because what we're about to move onto now depends massively on understanding the theory behind it.

We've already spoken about "sales funnels" and my dislike for the term. **Building profitable relationships with potential clients has nothing to do with "selling". It's purely about building belief.**

In the **Zero Leads** method, we use a very specific system of building belief, so we don't have to "sell".

And it's this system we're going to go through now, from start to finish.

The Belief Machine

This is the entire automated process that underpins the **Zero Leads** method, and it's made up of **5 distinct phases**:

1. The Acquisition Phase
2. The Indoctrination Phase
3. The Feedback Phase
4. The Discovery Phase
5. The Service Phase

Let's go through each phase and break down exactly what needs to happen in them:

The Acquisition Phase

This first phase is all about getting paying customers into your business. There are two ways to drive traffic to achieve that:

- **Organic methods** - blogging, social posting, community activity etc.

- **Paid methods** - social ads, banner ads, paid search, partnerships, affiliates etc.

Now don't be fooled. A lot of people mistakenly think that organic methods are free, so that's where they start, but nothing is "free".

Everything always has an opportunity cost. If you're writing blog articles or creating social posts yourself, then you're spending your time on it. Your time is never free and is arguably the most expensive asset you have. How much could you earn in project work during the time it took you to create organic content? What other, more important things (in and out of your business) could you be doing? That's your opportunity cost.

Don't get me wrong, I'm not saying don't go the organic route, I just want you to be aware of the misconceptions so you can make a more informed choice when you come to deciding.

There's only one difference between "paid" and "organic" methods, and that's speed. If you choose to buy ad space, then you can scale the amount of people that can come into contact with your business much quicker than with the organic route.

Over time, you can build organic traffic that sustains itself. You put the hard work in now for a few years and you'll continue to reap the benefits for years to come. That's the beauty of organic methods, they just take longer to pick up momentum.

Paid methods you can switch on and off like a tap. They are singular instances that only deliver traffic if you keep putting money into them. As soon as the money stops, your traffic stops.

Organic methods will always work out cheaper and have a higher ROI in the long run, but paid methods will grow your business faster. And with the **Zero Leads** method of offsetting your paid ad costs completely upfront, the expense is instantly removed and is no longer a cost to your business.

That's why, as part of the **Zero Leads** method, we use paid ads to scale businesses and see results quickly! You can still build organic content in the background for long-term sustainability if you choose, but paid ads are where the results are.

The platform doesn't really matter, Facebook, Google, YouTube, Pinterest, whatever. What does matter is making sure your ads are where your potential clients are, and you make more money than you spend on them. Remember the **Free Client Formula?**:

CPA < AOV = Guaranteed Profitable Growth

What you do need to have for an effective Acquisition Phase however is a really compelling offer, complete with order bumps and upsells, that your potential clients can (and want to) buy. We'll look into creating your **Signature Offers** in the next chapter.

This first phase majorly focuses on attraction - the entire first Quality of the **5 Connective Qualities** - the **Perceptive Connection** stage. You're targeting the emotional side of the brain with curiosity and impact.

Your branding and headline copy plays a massive part in being successful in this phase. And then you're backing it up by appealing to the rational side of the brain by introducing the benefit-driven features of your acquisition offers.

You're starting that journey of moving potential clients from the negative state they're currently in, to the positive state you know they're looking for.

You're starting to give them belief in the result, the method and you as a person/business to help them.

As a technical process, it's broken down into the following **6 components**:

1. Initial Offer Landing Page
2. Checkout Page
3. Upsell Offer 1 Page
4. Upsell Offer 2 Page
5. Thank You Page
6. Offer Delivery Email Sequence

The **Initial Offer Landing Page** is the first page they get to on your website from an ad that you've put out there. Its entire job is to position your low-barrier, low-cost offer as the solution to their problems. In *Chapter 10*, we'll be going through exactly what this offer should be and why. It includes images of the offer, a benefit-driven description and a button to "buy now".

Once they click the button, they're taken to the main **Checkout Page**. This page has all the usual fields to collect personal and payment details, but it also includes the "order bump" option that'll help balance the **Free Client Formula**. They can choose to add the order bump product to their order also, or decline.

Whichever option they choose, they're taken to the **Upsell Offer 1 Page**. This is another page similar to the **Initial Offer Landing Page** and has full offer images and a benefit-driven description of the upsell offer. Again, they have the option to add this first upsell offer or decline it.

Then they're taken to the **Upsell Offer 2 Page**, no matter their chosen option. This is the last offer page in the sequence and has a similar format to the previous page. Once more, they have the option to add this second upsell offer or decline it before completing their order fully.

This is a **One-Time-Only (OTO)** offer and should only be available on this page. That provides real urgency to add it to their order now. Note that this isn't the "fake" kind of urgency to trick people. This offer should really only be available on this page and nowhere else.

Once payment is made for all their choices, they'll be taken to the **Thank You Page**, which basically includes the order confirmation and next steps details so they can start with their purchases ASAP.

That's the end of the **Initial Offer Sequence** and is all website-driven.

Now that they're a paying customer, their details are passed through to your email system, where they're sent their purchases in the **Offer Delivery Email Sequence**. This automated sequence also delivers them further bonus content to continue building belief and trust.

The Indoctrination Phase

This is where one of the most important products you'll create comes in - **the book**.

The **Indoctrination Phase** is a beefy one and has a big job to do. If we think back to our relationship theory in *Chapters 6 and 7*, we're now hitting into the **Interest** and **Enlightenment Gates**. It's where we need to move our new customers and potential clients from being **Problem Aware**, to **Solution Aware** and moving into **Product**

Aware. It's also where the majority of the **Belief Continuum** must be thought about - building and changing their beliefs about the possibility of the end result and the methods to get there. The belief in you as a guide to help them get there. And the belief in themselves to actually have the ability to get there.

That's a lot of heavy lifting to be done, so we need something that has the best chance of doing that in the shortest time possible.

Enter, your book.

A book has the ability to do each of those incredibly effectively. If we think about it more closely, books are:

- The best way to demonstrate your knowledge, expertise and value up-front.

- A symbol of authority on a subject (who else could write 25-45,000 words on a single topic?).

- An incredibly effective way of initiating a relationship with someone and starting the belief change process (it's just you talking to them about their desires).

- A decent time investment, if someone reads it, they're serious about changing their future.

- Usually only read by those that want to invest in themselves and are more willing to invest money as well as time into their own personal improvement.

The book is a powerful and crucial part of the **Zero Leads** framework and is **the key to unlocking the revenue potential in your business.**

Your book is essentially where you take your potential clients on a journey - a journey that's specifically designed to pre-qualify them for your services.

Now this isn't just an empty sales pitch. That never works and would be a complete waste of your time to create and their time to read. This is a book packed with value that takes them through the following **4 sections**:

Section 1: Why does the reader need your offer?

This initial section should set the scene. It should go through your **Transformation Story** to build belief in you as a guide by going deeper into the **Character, Ethical, Relative** and **Momentum Connective Qualities**.

You'll also need to show them the benefits and "better life" they could have to build their belief in the method and result. And finally, you need to give them a way of evaluating their own businesses against the major, most common-place problems related to your offer, and where they could improve.

Section 2: What's your offer?

This is where you do a deep dive into the theory and tactics of your method. You need to provide solid foundations and facts to show them that your method is legit and proven to bring them the results they're looking for. Hard data is key here!

Section 3: How do they get their "first win"?

In the third section, it's time to get them started on their own journey. This is where you'll take them through one of the very initial steps in your method and show them exactly how to do it so they can start seeing results up front.

Section 4: What are their options to hit their goals?

Finally, now that they've started, it's about giving them realistic options to continue their journey to their desired result. This is where you'll be recommending your services, but in an honest and open way. This section should be balanced and fact-filled, so they have all the details they need to make an informed choice (whether it's your services they choose or not).

The second part of the **Indoctrination Phase** is the **Trust Building Sequence**. This is an ongoing sequence of emails that continues to build trust and belief even further. This is where you deliver tons of value up front and invite them to book a call with you to deepen your relationship further.

Now there're different opinions on the regularity of sending emails. Some say 365 days a year, others just when they have something to sell.

I don't like either of those approaches and like to set a balance between the two.

Now we need to send enough emails, so we stay "top-of-mind" with our potential clients, but not so much as to either piss them off, or just as bad, give them too much to read that they end up reading none of it at all!

Firstly, I stay away from sending emails on weekends. I don't want to think about work on a weekend, that's time for me and my family, so I don't want to intrude on other people's weekends either. That's just a personal view, however. There are many businesses that do send emails on the weekend (and is much more acceptable if you're in a B2C niche), so it really is down to your own values.

That leaves just weekdays, and personally, I find the "one-a-day" approach too much. I'm signed up to businesses that do this, and even though I enjoy what they send, I do end up missing more than I read which ends up forming an unintended habitual response of "it's ok to not open and read these emails" - which is definitely not a good behaviour to condition!

I prefer the **2-email approach** – Tuesdays and Thursdays. These are also the most popular days for opening emails, and it gives everyone a little room to breathe - including you! It's also enough to deepen a relationship with someone and build that trust we're after.

The Feedback Phase

The **Feedback Phase** kicks in after a certain period of time. Once they've made their initial purchases, you want to give them time to consume them properly **(the Indoctrination Phase)**. Directly after this is when you want their feedback. You want to know how they got on with everything. How useful they found it. Were there any areas that they needed more help on etc. This is where you build up your bank of testimonials and case studies…and you do it automatically.

This phase is made up of **2 parts**:

1. Testimonial Email Sequence
2. Testimonial Submission Page

First, your clients are sent a number of emails asking them for their feedback. People are usually reluctant to reply to requests for feedback in general, so we have to do repeat sends and frame in different ways to get them to take action.

Once they do, they're taken to a dedicated page that'll capture their thoughts. Now, the best place I like to capture testimonials is in a group post/comment. It's much less formal than some kind of website form, it can be replied to, sparking a two-way conversation, and it can also be seen instantly by other members of your community.

Testimonials are incredibly important in your business. They not only allow you to gauge the impact and success of your offers, but they also help build belief in future potential clients that see them. **Happy clients are the best salesforce you'll ever have.**

The Discovery Phase

The **Discovery Phase** is the "hybrid" part of the overall **Zero Leads** system. The initial stages are automated; however, it then leads into a one-to-one "Strategy Call" to find out more about the client, their challenges and goals, and to go through your options of how you can help them. It's based on this **5-stage process**:

1. Call Booking Page
2. Call Application Form
3. Call Scheduling Page
4. Call Booking Thank You Page
5. Strategy Call

The **Call Booking Page** is a very simple page. It basically lays out what the call is, what you'll go through in top-line detail, and what they'll come away with at the end of it. Finally an outline of next steps and the beginning of the next section…

The **Call Application Form** is a very important step within this process, and allows you to further pre-qualify your potential clients before you get on a call with them. This form should ask a few simple questions around your "acceptance criteria", i.e. what sort of business they are, what sort of clients they work with, what their monthly revenue is etc.. This will set you up nicely for the **Strategy Call** at the end of this phase.

Once they've filled in their questionnaire, they're taken to a page where they can book in a time slot for their 30-40 minute call with you.

Finally, they're taken to the **Call Booking Thank You Page** which confirms their call booking details and any next steps they need to take, including what happens now.

Next up is the actual **Strategy Call**. This is what everything's been building towards. You've now built enough belief in the result, you're also very close to building enough belief in you and in themselves. This call is the final, personal part of the puzzle that should solidify that belief, so they take the next step with you.

In general, the overall structure of the **Strategy Call** should look something like this **10-step process**. If you're covering each of these, then you're over half-way to a successful call:

1. Introductions
2. Pre-frame the call
3. Discover more about their business
4. Tell them more about your business
5. Good fit / bad fit
6. Options and investment
7. Objection handling
8. Ask for a decision
9. Technical details
10. Next steps & follow-up

The **Strategy Call** takes practice. **You have to *do* them to get better at them.** At first, you'll be shit. Don't worry about it, we all have to start somewhere. But you *will* get better.

Just remember, you aren't trying to "sell" to someone. You're simply trying to find out if you'd be the best person to help them. If it helps you, constantly be looking for reasons to say "no" to them. That'll automatically put you in the zone of listening and analysing rather than "pitching" and "selling". You're listening, diagnosing and prescribing, not trying to overwhelm, push and force your way onto them (it's not attractive…or very successful…).

The Service Phase

The name of this phase says it all really. This is when you start to deliver the service option that they've opted for. This phase can vary wildly depending on the services that you provide. And that's exactly what we're going to start looking at in the next Section of this book, starting with defining your **Unique Framework** in *Chapter 9*.

So now that we've gone through the practical structure of the **Zero Leads** system and you can see how everything flows through, let's tie that back to the theory that we learnt in *Chapters 6 and 7* to see how the entire system comes together:

Zero Leads Phases	Relationship Gates	Stages Of Awareness	Undesirable Negative States	Desirable Positive States
	-	Unaware		
Acquisition	Attraction	Problem Aware	Repulsion	Attracted
	Curiosity		Indifferent, aware	Fascinated, surprised
Indoctrination	Interest	Solution / Product Aware	Unmotivated, bored, fearful	Inspired, amused, hopeful
	Enlightenment	Most Aware	Anxious, lethargic, scared, doubtful	Anticipation, energised, courageous, confident
Discovery/ Service	Commitment		Pained, unfulfilled,	Relief, satisfaction,

			sadness, apathy	happiness, admiration
Feedback	Integration		Lowliness, disdain	Pride, worship

You'll notice that the **Feedback Phase** comes last theoretically, but in reality, we want to start asking for feedback as soon as possible. This Phase actually never ends, and the sooner you can get someone to give you positive feedback about their experiences and progress with your business, the faster they'll push themselves forward to trusting you and becoming a loyal client.

That's the entire **Zero Leads** method, laid out, from beginning to end.

It's not a complicated method. As we've spoken about previously, complexity kills success. The simplest things are the best things, because they can be understood by anyone, quickly and repeatedly implemented and easily scaled to achieve the type of growth you're looking for.

There're still a lot of things you need to get right in the system - the design, the images, the copy, the videos, the automations, the tech, the ad platform knowledge, the products, the services, the relationship building skills etc. And it's these things that separate an average system from a truly great system.

But overall, it's a simple method, designed to be implemented as quickly and effectively as possible so you can start seeing results as *quickly* as possible.

Key Takeaways:

- You're not in the job of "selling", you're in the job of building "belief". You need to be able to satisfy the 3 stages of the **Belief Continuum** with all potential clients to move them to take action with you. Belief in the result, belief in you to help deliver it and belief in themselves to be able to achieve it.

- To build belief, especially on a large scale, you need an automated system to help do it for you. This is where the **Belief Machine** comes in, and it's split into 5 Phases. **Acquisition, Indoctrination, Feedback, Discovery** and **Service**. Each of these Phases flow seamlessly into the next to effectively push your potential clients forward in their journey of belief.

- The overall system itself is simple. Simplicity scales, complexity doesn't. There're still a lot of elements to the system that work towards its overall success rate, but if you follow the 5 Phases, they'll lead you to more and better clients, increased revenue and less work on your part to make it all happen.

PART 3
CREATING YOUR SIGNATURE OFFER

9
HOW TO DEFINE YOUR UNIQUE FRAMEWORK

"Expertise is relative. We're all experts in the eyes of someone. Expertise is just another word for experience. If you have more experience in something than someone else, then you are their expert. It can be just one more thing you know. It can be a thousand. It doesn't matter. What matters is you know something they don't. You can help them achieve something they can't. You are an expert at something. An expert of your craft. Clients come to you because you are their expert. Have faith in your expertise. You can help them where they would be lost alone."

--

Nobody wants your services.

In all honesty, the only person that cares about your services is you.

Now that can be a bit of a "slap-in-the-face" the first time you hear it. I know it was for me. You're probably thinking (as I did), that your services are incredible, top quality, that you've poured so much effort, passion and attention into them to make them the best they can be. In fact, there's no other services that even come close…and they don't care?? How could they not care? Don't they understand the expertise and years of dedication and hard work it's taken to create them?

No. They don't. Only you do.

All your clients care about is a result. A change of state. A transformation.

They want to move away from the pains and challenges they're facing now to a better future where they're no longer having those issues.

But don't take it as a bad thing. Take it as the empowering realisation that it is. Very few freelancers understand this point and are stuck like a scratched record, droning on about their own services.

This is what now sets you apart!

Once you realise that no-one cares about your services, you can stop focusing on them and start focusing on what really matters - your clients.

People are willing to pay good money for good results, not good services.

Your services are merely a means to an end. They're the enabler of that result. Yes, they're still important, but only in their ability to effectively and efficiently get those results for them. The "how" matters much less when you're trying to win new clients.

Before we get into creating your "framework" we need to understand where its ultimate destination is. What's the overall purpose of it? Why does it exist?

The Transformation Matrix

This is where the **Transformation Matrix** comes in. A simple tool that I learnt from *Ryan Deiss, CEO of DigitalMarketer*, and it sums up the ideal result that your business exists to deliver.

It could be anything, and can be anything depending on your niche, ideal client and business type. It could be a million different things, but every **Transformation Matrix** has one thing in common, **they describe the results that are of highest value to your ideal client**.

It's made up of **2 main sections,** the "Before" section and the "After" section. This allows us to figure out where they are currently and where they desire to be (i.e. the transformation). These sections are split into 4 main categories, "Have", "Feel", "Average Day" and "Status".

Let's take a look at it visually:

	Before	After
Have		
Feel		
Average Day		
Status		

As an example, let me take you through the **Transformation Matrix** for the **Zero Leads** method. Here's what it looks like:

	Before	After
Have	Poor quality clients and a small list of "freeloader" leads.	A highly profitable stream of ideal, paying customers and clients from first contact.
Feel	Stressed, frustrated, trapped and depressed.	Happy, confident, motivated and energised
Average Day	Living in the "feast & famine" desperately clutching at new business (but not getting much).	Freedom of time and control to do whatever they want while business grows automatically.
Status	A "struggling failure"	The no.1 respected expert & authority in their niche.

Can you see how powerful this is?

It takes you away from "service" thinking and puts you firmly in the mind of your client.

This is the start of your business breaking free from the trappings of mediocrity. This is when you can start developing a true strategy of scale and growth that delivers massive value to your clients and transforms your life in the process.

Now that we understand the "end-goal", we can move onto the framework for delivering that desired transformation for our clients.

Your Unique Framework

Your **Unique Framework** is essentially the overall process. It's the steps that your client would need to take to achieve the end results listed out in the **Transformation Matrix**.

Keeping with the **Zero Leads** method, let's take a look at the basic overall framework for realising those results. It can be broken down into **5 simple steps**:

1. Define your "ideal" client
2. Create a unique, engaging brand
3. Design your product and service offers
4. Setup your automated sales machine
5. Attract your "ideal" clients

Within each step of the overall framework, there'll naturally be sub-frameworks that work together to achieve each one. For example, as we've touched on in *Chapter 7*, when looking at "creating a unique and engaging brand", the sub-frameworks look like this:

- Define your vision and mission
- Develop your values and promises
- Articulate your brand personality
- Create your tone of voice
- Finalise your visual design
- Write your "Transformation Story"

As you can see, if you take things step-by-step, you start to form a progressive structure of actions that need to happen in a particular order to get a defined result.

There're no mention of services just yet, just steps to a desired goal. Once we understand the full framework, then we can start thinking about "how" we'll deliver these to our clients - and there can be many ways to achieve the same thing, as we'll see in the next chapter.

You'll also notice that none of these points are new or groundbreaking. In fact, the general "tactics" are not my invention, and neither should you be "inventing" yours.

Creating something unique doesn't mean it needs to be something entirely new and never-before thought of in all parts. It's actually very rare that that's the case. **What makes something unique (yet still understandable and useful) is taking things that work and putting them together in a new way.** Or coming at something from a slightly different angle.

When you put your own twist and philosophy on something, that's when you stop being generic and start gaining traction.

One very powerful way of doing that is taking a commonly held way of doing something, altering it to make it work better and giving it a name or label. Just by the act of *naming* something, you can instantly make it unique and claim ownership. It's something your potential clients can't get from anywhere else - it's part of *your* **Unique Framework**.

If you think back through this book, you would've noticed that I have labelled lots of the frameworks I've introduced you to - **The Marble Run, The 6 Relationship Gates, The 5 Connective Qualities, The 7 Connection Maximisers, The Belief Continuum** and **Belief Machine** etc.

Now I didn't just have the epiphanies for these out of thin air. Each of them is a result of extensive reading and learning around the relative topics so I could form my own opinion and framework ideas. "Standing on the shoulders of giants" as it were - as we all should be doing, for that's how we progress and grow.

Labelling these frameworks not only associates them with me and the **Zero Leads** philosophy whenever you see them, they're also an easy way of recalling complex ideas.

When you've thought about all the steps your clients would need to do (if they were doing it all themselves) to achieve their desired results, you'll have your entire **Unique Framework**, complete with sub-frameworks.

Now it's time to make your ideas and business truly stand out!

The Irresistible Hook

We're going to come back to the principle of attraction. Remember, we're attracted to the new and novel, the things that build curiosity inside of us, the things that put our own existing beliefs into question.

In order to break through the noise of every other competitor in your niche, you're going to need to come up with something that snaps people out of their current routines and thought processes.

You're going to need an **Irresistible Hook**.

Now your "hook" is born from your overall philosophy about what you do and how you do it. It's essentially **an impactful summary of what your framework's all about**.

Let's come back to the example of the **Zero Leads** method. We've now been through the general framework, which isn't too dissimilar to other revenue-generating strategies out there, but there's a slight twist. This method goes against the common practice of "lead-generation".

Throughout my experience I've come to the conclusion that it can waste a lot of time and money for freelancers and can be a real pain point in their businesses. The rest of the "method" is pretty straightforward, but the way I position my framework is its **Irresistible Hook**.

It's something that's a major challenge and needs solving, and it's also a way of looking at things outside of the "norm".

I could've easily called the framework the "get thousands of clients" method, but it doesn't have the same pull, because that's what the rest of my niche is doing. It doesn't set me apart. It doesn't say that there's something more to my offer that's unique.

So just to recap then, your **Unique Framework** needs an **Irresistible Hook**, and the best ones come from the combination of 2 things:

- A real pain point that needs solving or desire that needs achieving.

- A contradictory standpoint that sets you and your philosophy apart in your niche.

Here are a few other genre-defining examples that have seen massive success:

The 4-Hour Work Week: Escape The 9-5, Live Anywhere And Join The New Rich – *Tim Ferriss*

This framework promises to condense a 40-hour work week into just 4 hours! Imagine all the free time you'd have? And not just that, think about what you'd do with all the extra money you'd be making from doing less work. All of this goes against the grain of the traditional working week concept.

Profit First: Transform Your Business From A Cash Eating Monster To A Money-Making Machine – *Mike Michalowicz*

The general way of doing things is that you take your profit last in your business after everything else. This framework turns that completely on its head. Imagine taking your profit *first* and still growing your business! This is a great concept that has sold millions of products & services off the back of it. And check out the title, not only does i mention the word "transform", it also explicitly states the "before" and "after" "Have" section of the **Transformation Matrix**!

The $100 Startup: Fire Your Boss, Do What You Love And Work Better To Live More – *Chris Guillebeau*

Startups traditionally cost a lot of money to set up, which put them out of reach for most people. But this framework lays out a method of doing it with just $100! Imagine needing only $100 to be able to get out of the job you hate and start living the life of your dreams! A very compelling prospect which drives the curiosity of "how".

Now these are the overall framework hooks. Within them there are dozens of other sub-frameworks that make up each method. As you may have noticed, each one of these is a framework and philosophy, but they're also book titles – exactly the same as **Zero Leads: The Secret To Growing A 7-Figure Freelance Business Without Any Leads**. We're going to move onto using a book as part of your offer strategy for your **Unique Framework** in the next chapter.

Key Takeaways:

- **People don't buy products and services, they buy results and transformation.** By using the **Transformation Matrix** we can determine what changes our ideal clients want in the things they "Have", the way they "Feel", their "Average Days" and the way they want to be seen by others – their "Status".

- Your **Unique Framework** is the **step-by-step process that someone would have to take to reach their desired transformation.** That framework will be made

- ...b-frameworks as the "method". Try not to think ...articular products and services you could offer ...ust the process of change to start with.

- Once you have your **Unique Framework**, you need an **Irresistible Hook**. This is something that'll separate your business from all your competitors in your niche. It's unique to you. **Your hook has to deliver on the promise of desired change and also has to build massive curiosity by going against the status quo.**

Exercise:

I want you to take the 3 concepts from this chapter and work on them for your business:

1. Think about your ideal client and complete a **Transformation Matrix** for them.

2. Thinking about their desired transformations and your skill set, what would be the key steps they'd need to take to achieve them? How could these steps be broken down further? This will become your underlying **Unique Framework**, complete with sub-frameworks.

3. Finally, I want you to think about your **Irresistible Hook** for your **Unique Framework**. What key point in your philosophy contradicts the "standard" way things are done in your niche? What are the resulting big benefit promises that your clients will achieve by using your **Unique Framework**?

10
THE FIVE FIGURE DROP

"Money alone is worthless. It's the potential of money that holds value. Money's purely a resource. A steppingstone, not an end goal. No-one wants more money to have more money. We want more money to effect more change. Money is a catalyst for change. The more money you have, the quicker you can make that change. Make a difference. What change will you make? What do you really need money for? Like any resource, we can use it wisely or waste it. Money is our chance to grow. To make our world better than it is today."

--

Time is our most valuable asset.

Some think it's money, but you can always get more money (there are millions of ways). **Money is infinite, time is not.**

We all have a certain amount of time on this planet, therefore it's the most precious thing we have. And it should also be the most reluctant thing we have to offer.

We need to choose where we spend our time with great care, to those people and causes that we can really make a difference to, and that can really make a difference to us.

In a business context, this concept can be summed up with what I call the **Time Pivot**.

The Time Pivot

Within any business relationship, there's you and your client. The **Time Pivot** principle is very simple:

- The **more direct time** you need to put in to achieve a result for them, the ***more* you charge**.

- The **less direct time** you need to put in to achieve a result for them, the ***less* you charge**.

From a client's perspective, it'll look like this:

- The **more time** they have to put in to achieve a result, the **less they pay**.

- The **less time** they have to put in to achieve a result, the **more they pay**.

You can see where these relate and the "pivot" aspect comes into play, right?

Basically, if the client's doing the majority of the work with only a little help from you, then they should be paying only a fraction of the cost than if you were doing all of the work, and they were doing very little.

Therefore, this concept opens the door to a sliding scale of time/effort and cost on the part of the client:

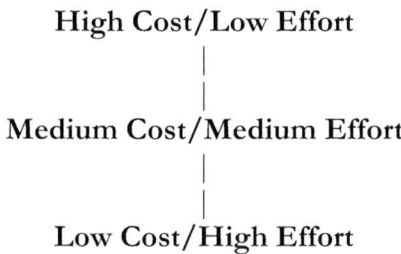

In the majority of service businesses, they solely focus on the **High Cost/Low Effort** area of the scale. These are the typical "done-for-you" services that all freelancers offer.

But as we can see, not everyone's looking for or wanting that level of service. All your potential clients are looking for the exact same result (that we figured out in the last chapter), but every single client will be at different stages and circumstances.

If you're only focusing on the **High Cost/Low Effort** clients, then you're missing out on over 2/3rds of your potential clients and revenue. You also need to have offers for the **Medium Cost/Medium Effort** clients and the **Low Cost/High Effort** clients.

This is where we can use the **Five Figure Drop** technique to figure out the 3 most important offers in your business, and to make sure you're not leaving money on the table.

The Five Figure Drop

If you're a freelancer providing a service and you're reading this (which I assume is the case), then you more than likely have a **High Cost/Low Effort** service that you already provide for your clients. You may even have more than one.

In order to maximise your revenue at every stage of the client journey and help as many people as possible improve their businesses and lives, we need to add two more offer categories to your business.

We've already briefly touched on these in *Chapter 7* when we went through the example of our mate Ben and the math of the **Free Client Formula**. The **Five Figure Drop** is how we work them out.

The **Five Figure Drop** is an awesome technique that's based on a concept I learnt from *Mike Killen, Founder of Sell Your Service,* as we randomly sat in this amazing farm shop eating freshly made bacon sandwiches and delicious, locally roasted coffee (that memory's making me hungry!). I've since adapted it to work better with the **Zero Leads** method, and it does two key things really well.

- Lays out your **3 Essential Offer Types** together so you can see the connections and flows between them.

- Gives you a method for determining your real product and service pricing.

The first point is a great thing to have, but it's the second point that's really valuable.

The majority of service business owners struggle when it comes to pricing. This technique helps clear all of that up by going about it "backwards". Instead of creating a product or service and asking yourself "how much should I charge?", you'll be asking yourself "what value can I deliver to hit these price points?".

Let's look at this a bit more closely:

The Five Figure Drop		
Offer Type	**Offer Cost**	**Offer Deliverables**
Service Offers - these are your full "done-for-you" services. They cater for the **High Cost/Low Effort** clients. These services aim to get the client the complete result in the quickest time and for the least effort on their part as possible. They're one-to-one and the least scalable.	$10,000 - $90,000	Creative services Project work
Guided Offers - these are your "done-with-you" products and services. They aim to help the **Medium Cost/Medium Effort** clients achieve their desired result, but with much less effort on your part. These are one-to-many and highly scalable.	$1,000 - $25,000	Online courses Coaching programs
Acquisition Offers - these are your introductory, trust-building products and focus on the **Low Cost/High Effort** clients. They're used to build knowledge and belief and should prepare clients to take the next steps with you. They're one-to-many and the most scalable.	$5 - $1,000	Books Audiobooks Workshops Mini courses Templates Tools

These are the **3 Essential Offer Types** you need in your business to target each type of potential client effectively - the **Acquisition Offer**, the **Guided Offer** and the **Service Offer**.

Each **Offer Type** is made up of different **Offer Deliverables** that satisfy that level of value, scalability and cost.

Your **Service Offers** should be made up of your full services to clients.

Your **Guided Offers** should consist of a combination of online courses and coaching programs as they're more scalable. These should both aim to deliver the same end result as your **Service Offers**, but with little-to-no direct input from yourself or your team.

And the **Acquisition Offers** are what you use to entice people into your business and will make up your initial offers, "order bumps" and "upsells".

As you may have worked out, this book that you're currently reading is part of my **Acquisition Offer**. It introduces you to me, my frameworks and methodologies, and my philosophies on business. It's also designed to start building belief in the results and method itself, me as someone who's experienced enough to help you achieve those results, and yourself having the ability to actually attain them.

If you purchased this book from my website, you would've also seen the rest of my **Acquisition Offers** in the form of my free bonus workshops and guides (which there are links to at the end of this book), and my "upsell" offers. These are positioned to help you start implementing what you've read in this book. They're more practical and move you forward towards your desired end goal of more quality clients, more revenue and less work.

These were all deliberately kept at a low cost as I want the barrier to entry to be as little as possible, but still covering my acquisition costs (just as we went through in *Chapter 7* and the **Free Client Formula**). The hope is that as you start interacting with me and my business more through my **Acquisition Offers**, you'll want to start working with us even closer to achieve the results I talk about in *your* business.

Each offer should flow onto the next and provide the "next logical step" for each and every potential client.

Now that we've looked at the offers themselves and how they're structured, I want to touch quickly on the pricing element. We're going to look at pricing in a completely different way than you've been taught before!

Backwards Pricing

This method of pricing is probably a little alien to you. Usually when we look at our pricing, we create something first and then work out how much we should charge for it. In the **Five Figure Drop** technique, we have our pricing levels first, and then we figure out what we could offer that would warrant those prices.

Starting with the **Acquisition Offers**, a book is the perfect option for the initial $5-10 price point. Audiobooks, single workshop videos and short templates can fall in the $30-$100 region, and short mini-courses in the $100 - $300 range, depending on the content. You can even include longer informational content here to scale up to the $1,000 mark if you wish.

Looking at the **Guided Offers**, the online courses should be full DIY options for your clients, whereas the coaching programs are the online courses with added personal feedback and group coaching sessions to help them through. The cost of an online course will be at the lower end of the cost scale ($500 - $5,000) and the group coaching programs should be at the higher end ($5,000 - $25,000).

The key to good group coaching programs is a specific length of time and a specific attainable result. You must be helping them work towards a specific goal by a pre-determined end point.

I've seen far too many coaching programs turn into a never-ending sequence of ongoing weekly/monthly calls that are more like a different form of content delivery, rather than direct help to achieve a specific result. Make sure yours has focus!

Finally, the **Service Offers**, at the lower end of this spectrum your offers will be "done-for-you" *sections* of your entire framework. At the higher end will be the entire framework done for them. Once you've figured out your overall **Unique Framework** that you offer, it should be easy to break it down into sections that you know your clients will want your help with.

There's a wide scale on the **Service Offer** pricing as it really does depend on the type of services you offer, the complexity of carrying them out and the value of the results you offer.

Please remember that when pricing your offers, people don't pay for the book, the course, the coaching program or even the service. What determines the price they'll pay (and therefore the deliverables you'll need to offer), are these **3 key aspects**, known as **The Value Triangle**:

1. The scale/probability of the end result

2. The speed of achieving that result

3. The client's desired level of involvement

These are all automatically taken into account in the **Five Figure Drop** technique, but I wanted to bring your attention to it so you're basing your deliverables on the right things and not just the "type" of deliverable.

The more transformational the end result (i.e. the bigger the gap between where they are now and where you'll get them to as part of their desirable goals), the more they'll pay. Likewise, if you can guarantee that result, then again, the more clients will be prepared to pay.

Speed is the next thing. If you can get them that result next week as opposed to next year, the more they'll pay. And as we've spoken about with the **Time Pivot** principle, the less effort they need to put in on their part, the more they'll pay for the privilege.

Key Takeaways:

- Time is our most valuable asset. **The more time you have to directly put into something, the more you should charge your clients**. This follows the **Time Pivot** principle that the less time you (and your team) spend on something, the more time your client will need to spend, and therefore should be cheaper to them. The less time they spend and the more time you invest, the more expensive that service should become.

- There are 3 types of client - those looking for **High Cost/Low Effort**, those looking for **Medium Cost/Medium Effort** and those looking for **Low Cost/High Effort**. Make sure you're targeting all 3 with the types of offers you're making. Don't leave money on the table by just having premium "done-for-you" services.

- The **Five Figure Drop** technique is a way of figuring out the **3 Essential Offer Types** you need in your business to hit all 3 client types. The **Acquisition Offers**, the **Guided Offers**, and the **Service Offers**. Each should offer the client access to the same end result but with varying degrees of time and help involved.

- Stop creating your services first and then trying to assign a price to them. Instead, start **Backwards Pricing**. Begin with the 3 levels of price ranges to hit the **3 Essential Offer Types** and determine what you could offer for each that your ideal clients would pay for. Remember that people don't pay money for things, they pay for results. The amount they'll pay depends on the

> scale/probability of the end result, the speed of achieving that result and their desired level of involvement. Factor these into your products and services correctly and you'll have a profitable **Signature Offer** structure at the heart of your business.

Exercise:

The offer creation stage of the **Zero Leads** method is integral to your profitability. It may take a bit of time to get it perfect but start thinking about it now and getting your ideas down.

There are 3 key exercises I want you to focus on for this chapter that'll kickstart your **Signature Offer** creation:

1. Take your **Unique Framework** that we developed in the last chapter and use it to fill out your **Five Figure Drop Service Offers**. Define you're complete "done-for-you" service, what your clients will get, and how much you'll charge. From there, work out the "sections" of your **Service Offers**. What will they deliver and how much will they cost?

2. Next, I want you to start thinking about breaking your **Unique Framework** up as a selection of courses. What would each of those courses be about? What order would they go in? What would you teach in each of them?

3. Finally (and most importantly) I want you to start planning your book. What would the overall structure

> be? What main points do you want to tell your new customers about? The quicker you start on your book, the sooner everything else will start falling into place.

We Can Help:

These exercises can seem a little daunting, especially if you don't know where to begin. But that's where my team and I can help. We help motivated freelancers like you figure out their **Unique Frameworks** and **Essential Offers**. We help them plan and structure their premium courses based off those frameworks. And we guide them through the entire process of writing their own book (even if they've never written anything before), as part of our 14-day method (the very same 14-day method I used to write and publish this book!).

If you'd like us to help you with any of the above, just book a call with us at the link below and we can have a quick chat about your own goals, challenges and come up with a plan of action to grow your client base and monthly revenue.

We *seriously* get excited about this stuff and love helping creative freelancers instantly make a real difference in their businesses.

www.growthquadrant.co/call

11
HOW TO COME UP WITH IRRESISTIBLE PRODUCT IDEAS

"Growth doesn't happen through luck. It's not about being there at the right time. Growth happens when you have alignment. Growth happens when you have balance between passion, skill and desire. You must have passion for what you do to keep going when times are tough. You must have the skill to carry it out. And there must be a desire for what you offer. A desire strong enough to make your efforts worthwhile. Miss any one and growth will be hard. Balance all three and growth is inevitable."

--

The products and services that you offer should simply be a reflection of your ideal clients' challenges and desires.

Unfortunately, a lot of businesses create their products based on other things entirely - their own interests and abilities. A particular tool they have access to. Because their mum thought it was a "lovely idea".

This is where they miss the mark. To come with product ideas that are absolutely irresistible to your ideal clients, that they just "have to have", you need to understand the following process I'm about to take you through.

Every product and service (and piece of content) you create in your business should always satisfy the **5 Creation Questions**:

1. What pain is it solving?

2. What question is it answering?

3. What belief is it changing?

4. Is it the "next logical step"?

5. How does it help get the result quicker and easier?

Let's start with the first question and work our way down…

Question #1: What Pain Is It Solving?

We've already gone through the Transformation Statement. The pain, challenge or obstacle is the fundamental basis to any help or advice you give. If you don't explicitly know the pain you're trying to solve, how can you accurately offer a remedy that works?

Question #2: What Question Is It Answering?

Attached to any pain or problem are questions. These questions are what your potential clients will have in their minds. It's our natural way of looking for a solution, so we search for answers.

Every potential client comes to you with a Level Of Knowledge of your area of expertise and a Level Of Implementation of that knowledge in their business. These levels can each be broken down as follows:

Level Of Knowledge:

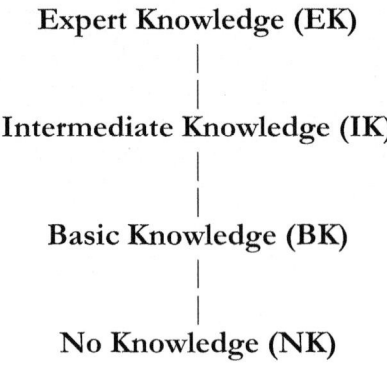

Level Of Implementation:

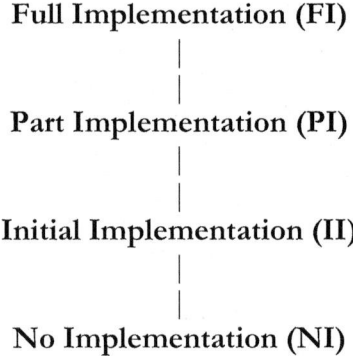

Depending on which Level your potential client's at, different questions will be racing through their minds. The products and services you create will be meeting people at these different levels, so you need to understand the questions they'll be searching for answers for.

When we put them together, their questions will be based around the following themes:

	NI	II	PI	FI
NK	Where do I begin?	-	-	-
BK	How do I do the first step?	What're the next steps of the process?	-	-
IK	How do I setup the whole system in my business?	How can I fast-track the system setup?	Who can give me help and guidance to complete my system properly?	-
EK	Who can setup my entire system for me?	Who can complete my system for me?	Who can check my system?	How do I take my results to the next level?

You can see how the nature of the questions change as the Levels increase, **from information-seeking to resource-seeking**. Those who don't have the knowledge, want to know. And those that have the knowledge want someone else to do it for them (usually because they don't have the time themselves to do it, so they outsource it).

Therefore, when you're positioning your products and services, think about where they fit into these Levels. Within each Level, you can obviously become more specific as well. The more specific you are, the more you're likely to convert a potential client into a paying client.

The best way to "know" your ideal clients' questions is to *ask* them. If you have access to them through clients that you work with already or groups and communities you're a part of, send them an email, put up a post and ask them what questions they have right now. What's stopping them from progressing? Where're they getting stuck?

The second-best way to "know" your ideal clients' questions is to "stalk" them. Not in a weird way (definitely not part of the **Zero Leads** method). More in the sense of being where they are and reading the comments and questions that they post.

A great way of doing this is to create a list of what I call **Connection Catalysts**. These are figureheads within your niche that are already attracting your ideal clients to them. I'm talking about social influencers, video channels, websites, blogs, forums, groups and communities etc. All the biggest and key places your ideal clients are hanging out. Check out the type of content that's being created. What questions are they answering? What questions are being asked? Aim for your top 100 **Connection Catalysts** and make it a habit of being part of, reading and participating in all of them. Every single answer to every question you have is there somewhere.

Question #3: What Belief Is It Changing?

We've talked about the importance of the **Belief Continuum**. The concept of building belief in the result and system, building belief in you as a guide and building belief in themselves of the possibility for change.

A great product will naturally do all three simultaneously. By the very act of you offering something that'll progress them and get them closer to their ultimate desired result, you'll be building belief in the validity of your system and framework, you'll be building their trust and belief in you to help them (because you are helping them*)*, and as they start to see results from using your products and services, they'll believe in their own ability to effect change.

As you create your products and services, keep this in mind, and think about how well they can influence all three areas of belief.

Question #4: Is It The "Next Logical Step"?

We've kind of hinted at this in the **Level Of Knowledge** and the **Level Of Implementation** point previously, but it's worth calling out explicitly this time.

The very best product or service is always the "next logical step" in a client's journey to achieving their desired end result.

Think about where they currently are. What do they know? What have they done with that knowledge? Those two answers will give you a massive clue as to where to go next with your offers.

Very rarely do people want everything all at once. We want things broken down step-by-step, and the more you offer it to people that way, the more likely they are to request your help, and actually succeed in reaching their goals.

Question #5: How Does It Help Get The Result Quicker And Easier?

This final point is based on something that I call the **Quick & Easy Principle**. It's a concept that follows on nicely from the **Time Pivot** that was introduced in *Chapter 10* (and not based on my college years as some might think…).

As a species we're lazy. We want results. We want them now. And we don't want to have to work for them. As a default setting, that's about as "human" as it comes. So, it goes without saying then that **the quicker and easier you can make achieving a specific result, the more desirable your offer becomes.** And as we know, the quicker and easier you make it for them to get to their ideal end result, the more valuable it becomes and the more you can charge for the privilege.

As you create new products and services, think about how "quick and easy" you're making something. You're naturally going to create different products and services that meet people at different levels of their knowledge and implementation journeys. As you sort out the "next logical step", think about the level of effort involved on your client's part and create a range of options to achieve that same result.

Some people will want to do everything themselves; they'll just want to know "how". Others will want you to do everything for them, and they'll happily pay. But there'll be a wide spectrum in between of people that want help with specific parts of the process and not others.

Think about all the tangible results that you aim to deliver with your service. How can you make each tangible result easier and quicker to achieve? These "processes" or "templates" or "courses" or "done-for-you services" will naturally sort themselves out into great product offer ideas.

Key Takeaways:

- Every product and service you create should be born from the challenges and desires of your ideal client. There should be no other reason. It doesn't matter if you want it, or someone else has asked for it, **if it doesn't help your ideal client progress to the desired end result, don't do it.**

- When you're creating something for your business, ask yourself the **5 Creation Questions** - What *pain* is it solving? What *question* is it answering? What *belief* is it changing? Is it the *next logical step*? How does it help get the result *quicker and easier*?

Exercise:

In this exercise, you're going to come up with a range of product and service ideas that you could potentially use in your business.

Now you might not necessarily use all of them but knowing all of them will give you a great insight into what could work at each point of their journey with you.

1. Create your top 100 **Connection Catalyst** list and start looking for general pains, challenges, barriers and questions that your ideal clients have. Make a list of the recurring trends you see.

2. Look at your overall **Unique Framework** process. Make a list of all the tangible results that you offer your clients. Each one of these step-by-step results can easily turn into a product, or selection of products.

3. With your list of tangible results, think about how you can keep delivering each result quicker and more easily (on their part) to the client. Use these ideas to create a suite of products at the increasing price points we discussed as part of the **Five Figure Drop**.

JAMES BRAY

PART 4
THE BUSINESS OF BELIEF

12
HOW TO MAXIMISE CONVERSIONS (AND PROFIT)

"Happiness equals money. It's not the other way round. Yes, money can buy things. Money can buy experiences. Money can buy pleasure. But money can't buy happiness. However, happiness can buy money. True happiness comes from the relationships we build, the people we help and support. The community we're a part of. The more we fill our lives with these things, the happier we become. Money then, is a potential bi-product of happiness. Productise your happiness. Build a service from your heart. And let your happiness gift you wealth."

--

Once you have your **Zero Leads** system up and running, the next (and ongoing) job is to make sure it's delivering the best results possible for you.

This is where the extremely important idea of **Conversion Rates** comes into play.

Conversion Rates are probably the most important metric I look at whenever I'm working on my own business or the businesses of my clients. They give an incredibly accurate picture as to what's working in a business and what's not.

They're essentially "transition metrics", from one stage of the client journey to the next. **Conversion Rates** are measured in percentages, and the higher the percentage, the better.

Here are the **10 Conversion Points** within the **Zero Leads** method and the relevant factors that affect the Conversion Rate at each point:

1. Ad To Initial Offer Landing Page

This first point is all about the ad itself. You'll want to look at the imagery used, the headline, the ad copy, the CTA button text and the targeting to increase your conversions here.

2. Initial Offer Landing Page To Book Purchase

This is all about the **Initial Offer Landing Page**. You'll want to look at the page design, page load speed, the headline, the offer copy, the offer contents, the offer price and imagery used to increase your conversions here.

3. Order Bump Purchase

This is all about the order bump callout. You'll want to look at the headline, the main copy, the offer contents and the offer price to increase your conversions here.

4. Upsell 1 Purchase

This is all about the **Upsell 1 Offer Page**. You'll want to look at the page design, the headline, the offer copy, the offer contents, the offer price and imagery used to increase your conversions here.

5. Upsell 2 Purchase

Same as with the **Upsell 1 Offer Page**, you'll want to look at the page design, the headline, the offer copy, the offer contents, the offer price and imagery used to increase your conversions here.

6. Email Open Rates

This is purely to do with the email subject line and the email deliverability. Or in other words, does it go to the junk or inbox? And when it gets there, does the subject line entice them to open it?

7. Email Click-Through Rates (CTRs)

Email CTRs get a little bit more involved. You'll want to look at the topic, the offer, the CTA copy and the CTA design to increase your conversions here.

8. Customers To Call Bookings

This point is all about your email CTAs and your **Call Booking Page.** You'll want to look at the CTA copy, positioning, design and frequency of your emails. You'll also want to look at the design and content of your **Call Booking Page** itself - the headline, body copy, the service options you offer and the application form process to increase your conversions here.

9. Call Bookings To Clients

This is down to your **Strategy Call**. You'll want to look at your confidence levels, your clarity, your ability to ask the right questions, to summarise succinctly, to build trust through your knowledge and demeanour, your call process and your end-of-call CTA. This is the part that takes the most practice, but with enough calls under your belt, it gets much, much easier.

10. Testimonial Acquisitions

This is down to the way you request your testimonials. You'll want to look at your emails - how often you request, the timing of your requests and the wording of your requests. You'll also want to look at the form you use to capture feedback, the longer it is, the lower it'll convert.

Let's put all of this into a basic example.

Here's a list of those same **Conversion Points** with average **Conversion Rates** you'd see and the number of customers/clients that would convert. We'll start with 1000 visitors to the **Initial Offer Landing Page** and start from there:

Conversion Point	Average Conversion Rate	No. Of People
Ad To Initial Offer Landing Page	3%	1000
Initial Offer Landing Page To Book Purchase	40% (of 1000 people)	400
Order Bump Purchase	15% (of 400 people)	60
Upsell 1 Purchase	7% (of 400 people)	28
Upsell 2 Purchase	2% (of 400 people)	8
Email Open Rates	20% (of 400 people)	80
Email CTRs	2% (of 400 people)	8
Customers To Call Bookings	10% (of 400 people)	40
Call Bookings To Clients	40% (of 40 people)	16
Testimonial Acquisitions	30% (of 400 people)	120

The conversion rates outlined in this table are a general guide, they can be much higher, but if you're looking for something as a baseline to measure up against, this'll deliver you a pretty healthy business.

If you're quite a way off these, then you have some work to do at the **Conversion Point(s)** in question. Go back up to the areas you need to look at and see where you could most likely improve. It'll then be time to test, test, test and run with the winners.

The Conversion Triangle

While you can (and will) dig down into the detail above to optimise your **Zero Leads** system, I want to zoom out here for a second. It's very easy to get caught in the nitty-gritty of everything. And when that happens, you become blinkered to the overall situation.

All conversions are essentially based on **3 factors**, and these 3 factors make up **The Conversion Triangle**:

1. The Spark
2. The Belief
3. The Offer

Let's take them in order and go into a little bit more detail on each one:

The Spark

The very first thing is the part that grabs their attention. We're bombarded with thousands of different messages a day. Yours' needs to stand out above the rest. **It needs to stop your potential client in their tracks and get them wanting to know more.**

Curiosity and the promise of results are crucial here. Remember, it needs to appeal to our brain's "emotional gatekeeper" - the Limbic System. It needs to be new, novel, impactful and different. It has to be the right thing at just the right time for them. And that's why you need to get both your message and your timing right to "spark" the fire in someone to learn more about you, your business and what you have to offer.

The Belief

How well are you satisfying all 3 stages of the **Belief Continuum**? Do they fully believe in the result and method of getting to their desired end result? Do they fully believe in you as their potential guide? Do they believe in themselves and their own ability to achieve it?

You can increase belief with more empathy, honesty, clarity and passion. **The more you believe it, the more it'll pass on to them.** And even better, the more you can prove it through the actual results of others, the more they'll believe it can work for them too.

The Offer

The final part of the **Conversion Triangle** is the offer itself. Now the offer isn't your product or service - they're just the methods by which you deliver results. The offer is the result itself. And to get people to act, you need to make the offer a "no-brainer".

The value of the offer should be around 10x more than the price that you're asking for it. **The larger the positive gap in value, the more conversions you'll see. The closer it gets, the less your offer will convert.** And if it drops into negative territory (i.e the price you're asking is more than the value you're delivering), then it won't convert at all.

Remember that value is relative, however. What might be valuable for one audience may not be to another. What might be expensive to one audience may not be to another. That's why it's critical that you fully understand the target client you're aiming for and position it to them as a "can't miss opportunity".

Whenever you're not where you want to be with your conversion rates, I want you to think about it in terms of **The Conversion Triangle**. Do you create enough of a spark? Do you build enough belief? Do you offer enough value?

If you come at it from this angle every time, you'll start seeing your **Conversion Rates** increase automatically. And as your **Conversion Rates** increase, so will your profits along with them.

Key Takeaways:

- **Conversion Rates** are "transition metrics". They measure the rate at which potential clients work their way through each part of your **Belief Machine**. They're the most important metric to keep an eye on in the **Zero Leads** system as they'll tell you exactly where you're knocking it out of the park and where you need to up your game a little more.

- Overall, the **Zero Leads** method has **10 Conversion Points**. Each of these points will determine the number of clients you start working with and the amount of revenue you start bringing in. There're various things you can tweak at each point to improve the **Conversion Rate**, but if you start by aiming for the baseline averages, you'll be in a pretty decent position to grow from there.

- All conversions are dependent on **The Conversion Triangle**. There needs to be enough of a spark created to hook people in. There needs to be enough belief built around the result, method, you and in themselves.

And there needs to be enough value in the offer that you're making. Whenever you're trying to get a potential client to act on something, keep these 3 things in mind and make sure you're covering all of them in equal measure.

13
BUILDING YOUR ZERO LEADS TEAM

"There's only one thing we can't get any more of. No matter how hard we try. There's only one thing that we're constantly losing. No matter how much we wish it wasn't so. Time is the most precious thing we have. To make the most of time is to make the most of life. Don't work to make more money. Work to make more time. That should be your ultimate goal. Make time to be there for others. Make time to be there for yourself. Make time for happiness. For what's life without it? Time is your best asset...you'll miss it when it's gone."

--

I hope that what I've covered in this book has inspired you to adopt the **Zero Leads** method in your business. To start taking control of your client numbers and quality, your revenue intake and your levels of profitability and growth.

We've been through a lot in this book, and although overall the process is a relatively simple one, there are still a lot of moving parts that come together to form the whole.

I've worked at this for over 15 years, slowly building my skills and abilities in each area of the system - offer strategy and pricing, branding, book creation, course creation, copywriting, web design, video production, email automation, paid ad management, content creation, data analytics etc. I've literally spent every working day over that time developing these aspects so I could implement them effectively together and build out my **Unique Framework**.

When you start on your own **Zero Leads** journey, you'll naturally be amazing at some of those things, breezing through them and cranking out results. However, there'll always be areas where you come up against obstacles and roadblocks. All the motivation and the desire in the world can come to a halt when you can't see a way forward.

But that's ok. In these situations, you basically have **2 options**:

Option #1: Learn how to do it by yourself

This is the slowest of the two options.

Like I said, I've taken this route over the last 15 years or so to gain all the knowledge and skills I need to be able to implement these tactics successfully.

It takes a lot of time, effort, patience and failure before you start dialling everything in. Essentially, it's learning by doing – trial and error. You'll hopefully get there eventually, but remember, our most valuable asset is time. And this is the quickest way to eat into the time you have.

It's also the best way of leaving money on the table – your opportunity cost. Let's say it takes you 5 years to figure it all out alone, think about all of the clients you *could've* helped in that time. All of the money you *could've* made. The life you *could've* been living…

I went down this path, and although I'm there now, I wouldn't recommend it!

Option #2: Get someone else to tell you exactly what to do

This is the quickest of the two options, and the easiest for you.

Find a coach or mentor, someone that has solid experience in doing this before. Someone that can show you exactly what you need to do next and point out where you can improve to get the best results possible.

Knowing what I know now, if I'd had the option of a great coach 15 years ago, I would've jumped on it! I would've seen results 100x faster with much less time (and money) wasted on trial and error.

A coach may seem like a "big expense" at the time, but trust me, the amount of value and speed of results they bring is well worth the initial outlay (100 times over to be honest!).

The beauty of this option is that you're guaranteed the best results in the shortest time possible because you've got top people working with you on YOUR business - people that do this day-in, day-out. It's their "bread and butter". They know the best ways of achieving the goals you've set for yourself, they know all the potential pitfall areas and effective workarounds. They know how everything fits together and what each stage and component needs to have to deliver the best results.

When looking at the **Zero Leads** method, there're **2 main areas** that you'll likely need help in:

1. Productising your service and offers
2. Building your **Belief Machine**

Let's take a closer look at the products side of things first, and then we'll delve into the **Belief Machine** after.

ZERO LEADS

14
GETTING STARTED WITH YOUR PRODUCTS

"Stop procrastinating. Don't fear what comes next. The time is never right. Will never be right. So now is better than any. You don't have anything more important to do. Shut out the distractions. Consider preparations done. You'll fail, but you'll learn. And you won't learn unless you try. You'll carry on pushing forwards. If you just start. Life's too short for hesitation. Don't let time steal your achievements. Do it and do it now. You'll thank yourself later. It's time to begin, the world is waiting for you."

--

When it comes to the products side of the **Zero Leads** method, you're going to need to create **3 types**:

1. Books

2. Templates

3. Courses

Each of these product types have different skills, requirements and costs associated to them.

Let's start with the book.

Creating Your Book

This is the product that attracts your ideal clients and introduces them to your **Unique Framework** and your business and life philosophies. Arguably the most important part of your product suite!

A lot of people love the idea of writing a book, but never do it. They're worried that they won't know what to write, couldn't write enough to fill a "whole" book, or won't have the time (because it will "take ages").

I want to let you in on a little secret. Do you want to know how long it took me to write this book?

14 days.

Just 14 days to write, edit, format, design the cover and publish. This is my first book, and I did everything myself. And let me tell you, I'm nothing special. I also had those initial thoughts that were preventing me from starting. It's natural. But I then made a mental commitment to myself, and I put a process in place.

I wrote on average 4,000 - 5,000 words a day. Just to put that into context, that's only 2 good blog posts. That's also around my other work in my business and being a father to two young children, making the family breakfast, doing the school runs, getting dinner ready, bath & bedtime etc.

I'm not super-human. Just dedicated. And that's what it takes to do it (and anything in life and business)…dedication. Dedication to carry on each day and make it a habit. Dedication to seeing it through and getting it done no matter what.

If you want to get started writing your book yourself, we can help guide you through the entire 14-day process, so at the end of it, you'll have your book published and bringing in new clients for you. Just book a call with us here and let's have a chat about your goals and challenges, so we can come up with a plan of action together:

www.growthquadrant.co/call

We'll give you a simple framework and full support so you can do everything yourself, quickly and easily.

To put it into perspective however, let's say you were to outsource your book creation (or parts of it…). You would need to hire a "book production team" of the following people. As you'll see, the costs start to add up for the individual parts of the process.

In fact, at the top end, you'd be looking at around $38,150…and even at the low end it would be around $23,300!

These costs are based on a 100-150 page book of between 25,000 - 35,000 words:

	Your Book Production Team	
Ghost-writer / Assistant Writer	Will write all or parts of the book for you. You give them the ideas; they'll turn them into a book. Make sure you're hiring a proven professional however.	$20,000 - $30,000
Editor	Will look at the overall flow and structure of your text. They'll advise how to order your text and where to cut for maximum readability and understanding for your readers.	$1,000 - $3,000
Proof-reader	Will look over the final draft for any spelling mistakes and grammatical errors. Don't neglect the small things. Books	$500 - $1,500

	with typos still sell, but your authority will take a hit every time your readers come across a mistake.	
Formatter	Will design the inside of your book - the contents page, chapter headings, page numbers etc. They can also provide you with the pdf, epub and/or mobi files for e-readers and print publishing.	$50 - $150
Designer	Will design the book cover, spine and back cover artwork. They can also create mock-up visuals for your website and social ads etc.	$250 - $500
Voice Artist	Will read through your book creating an audio track(s) for audiobook usage.	$1,000 - $2,000
Audio Editor	Will take the audio track(s) and edit, enhance the levels, look at the noise reduction and add any music you may require to complete the audiobook file. They'll output into mp3 format.	$500 - $1,000

Creating Your Templates

This is probably the easiest product type to create out of the three, because you're already creating something like them as part of your project work.

Knowing what to create as a template and how to package them up into your **Signature Offer** will take a bit of thought (although it's something that we've already been through in *Part 3* of this book).

The main challenges here, especially for non-designers is making things look good, on-brand and professional. Also the creation of promotional mockups etc.

Again, these are all areas we can support you with, to get them done in the shortest time possible, with the least amount of effort and have your assets look incredible.

Creating Your Courses

As amount of work and effort goes, this is probably on par with creating your book, just some of the skills required are a little different.

If you think about it, your course(s) will be very similar to your book - going through a method or framework, breaking down each point and introducing further detail around the "what, why and how".

Whereas your book will focus on your entire **Unique Framework** from a birds-eye view, your course(s) will go into the individual sub-frameworks within it, teaching people the exact "how-to". The key difference outside of level of content is in the presentation.

Courses are usually made up of the following main elements:

- Video lessons

- Presentation slides

- Lesson transcriptions

- Lesson audio files

- Worksheets

- Course platform

- Optional coaching element

After the initial strategy and planning stages of designing a course (looking at topic, content, learning points and structure), you'll need to get creating. Having created hundreds of course materials over the years, we have a solid, step-by-step process that we can support you through. This process has been finely honed to put together the best courses in the quickest time possible.

Again, if you were looking to outsource this however, here's who you'd need for your "course production team" and what you'd be looking to pay. It ranges from around $7,700 to $14,500 – and that's minus the monthly coaching costs.

This is roughly based on a 6-hour course:

	Your Course Production Team	
Graphic Designer	Will take care of all the design work necessary for the course, including presentation slide design, worksheet design, course banners and any promotional design assets.	$2,000 - $4,000
Content Writer	Will take the framework you provide and write a script for each lesson.	$500 - $1,000
Voice Artist	Will take the finished script and record the lesson voice tracks.	$1,000 - $2,000
Motion Designer	Will animate logo intros and end slates for your videos.	$100 - $500
Video Editor	Will take the lesson voice tracks and combine with the presentation slides and motion designs into full videos. They'll also output the lessons into mp4 format ready to be	$1,000 - $1,500

	uploaded to your course platform. They should also be able to output mp3 files of just the lesson audio.	
Transcriber	Will create and check over the lesson recording transcriptions and work into text that's easy to read (without "ums and ahs" etc.) and make sure the words on the recording have been captured accurately.	$600 - $1,000
Course Developer	Will take care of all the background tech including video hosting, site hosting, the course platform, payment gateways etc. They'll build out your courses with the lesson assets they're given.	$2,500 - $4,500
Coach	Will take on regular live coaching sessions (weekly, monthly etc.) to your course program students. They'll develop the session content and work with students answering their questions etc.	$100 - $1,000 / month

As you can see, it can end up costing quite a bit – especially once you add that to the book creation costs…

Just for a few of the products you would need, you'd be looking at spending anywhere from $31,000 to $52,650.

That's a lot of money, especially as a freelancer trying to get more clients and more revenue in the door!

I want to give you an honest breakdown of where I think your money's best spent. The "learn by yourself, do it yourself" is the cheapest option initially, but will end up costing you more in missed opportunity clients and revenue over the time it takes you to fail your way to success.

The "outsource everything" option is great if you've already got tons of money in the bank and no time to do anything.

But as you're reading this book, I'm going to assume that you don't have the desire for the first option or the resources for the second.

That leaves the happy middle-ground.

Now I'd *love* for you to become a coaching client of mine, I won't lie. We live for helping creative freelancers quickly systematise their sales and marketing to bring in more monthly clients and grow their revenue on autopilot.

And that's the key here really. Speed.

Yes, you can most definitely try and learn to do everything yourself, it'll just take much, much longer. Why delay the gifts you have and the value you can bring to the world? Your potential clients need you now! They want your help now. Surely, it's better to work with them and get them awesome results as quickly as possible? They win quicker, and you win quicker. The time to grow is now!

Let's have a chat about where you are now, where you want to be, and figure out a way of getting their together. Book in your free call with us at the link below.

www.growthquadrant.co/call

15
GETTING STARTED ON YOUR BELIEF MACHINE

"If all you do is take, you fail. If all you do is give, you fail. There must be balance. There must be something in it for all. Every instance should be an equal exchange. As soon as there's imbalance, there's frustration. There's anger, envy and scorn. There's a growing shadow of injustice. What works for you must work for the other. And vice versa. As you go into your next conversations, ask yourself what they need. What you need. How can you both come out with what you want? How can you both win?"

--

Here's the bottom line…

Creating your products is actually the easy bit and something you should definitely be doing. You're the subject matter expert. You're the one that wants to build a relationship and rapport with your ideal clients. So, you should be the one filtering as much of your knowledge and personality into your products as possible.

The best thing you can do with your products is invest in a guide/mentor to coach you through the process. In that way you know with certainty that you're on the right track and you're not wasting any of the time, effort and money you put in.

I want to highlight one of the most important points in business to you now:

People don't buy into products and services, they buy into belief.

To break this down a little further, the actual quality of your products and services doesn't have any effect on the number of sales you make. How could it? Your potential clients don't have access to or experience them until AFTER they've paid you. That means you "could" have shit products and services and still sell them (although I wouldn't recommend it…not if you actually want to keep your clients and gain great testimonials).

But that doesn't work the other way round.

You could have the best quality products and services in the world, but **if you do a bad job at building belief with your potential clients, you'll struggle to sell anything.**

Building your **Belief Machine** in the right way however is key to the success of your business, and it's an entirely different story to creating your products. There's a huge amount of specific technical skill and expertise needed in creating a machine that delivers results.

Where I would generally recommend a mentor to guide you through the product creation process, I would say having a coach is absolutely essential for building out your Belief Machine.

Now you're probably thinking, "well James, of course you'd say that, because you'd like me to pay you to help me do it", and yes, you'd be right. I'd love to help you build out your **Zero Leads** system and **Belief Machine** fully…it's the whole reason I wrote this book (not for fun, as some may guess).

But in all seriousness, whether you work with me and my team, or go elsewhere to get help, it doesn't really matter. The main thing I want to make sure of is that you're not wasting your time, effort and money where you don't need to.

Trust me, it'll take you years to figure out the ins and outs of building a successful system - it took me years - and it's my full-time profession! I don't want that for you (and you shouldn't really want that for yourself either).

To give you a clearer view, here's everything that you'd need to build a successful "machine" that consistently delivers great results:

- Sales copy for ads, offer pages, upsell video scripts, thank you pages etc.

- Nurture email copy that builds trust and belief in your initial customers and turns them into paying clients.

- Email automation setup with templates and conditional flow logic.

- Website setup with offer pages and thank you pages etc.

- Cart and payment gateway setup to enable "order bumps" and "upsells" etc.

- Full integrations between ad platform, website, email platform, payment gateway and course platform.

- Ad setup and ongoing management.

- Campaign analysis, optimisation and scaling.

- Consistent brand design across emails, website, ads and videos.

- Etc.

As you can see, it's a much more complex task to get everything built and working together.

As we've already briefly mentioned, there are **3 options** available to you then:

Option #1: Go It Alone:

If you still want to take it on yourself, be prepared for it to take a lot longer, require more effort and allow costs (both time and money) for learning and mistakes along the way.

Just be warned however: there're a million and one different ways to write sales copy, to setup paid ads, to build email automations etc. But there's a specific way of doing so that works for *this* method. **Only learn from those that understand what you're trying to achieve.**

Option #2: Invest In Guided Help:

This is a massive step up from scouring random YouTube videos and blog posts, trying to piece everything together and figure it all out by yourself.

This is being able to speak directly with the experts that do this each and every day. It's about being told exactly what you need to do, how you need to do it and then getting real-time feedback on your implementation – specifically for YOUR business.

We offer a program where our clients can work with me and my team to get step-by-step support, feedback and results across everything in this system. We aim to get you to 5-figure months in 90 days.

Coaching is the best option for people that want the most amount of help for the least upfront investment, while still achieving great results.

Our coaching option is a fraction of the cost of what the full "done-for-you" services come in at (as you'll see below).

Option #3: Hire Someone To Do It All For You:

Finally, you can outsource everything and let the experts do it for you. This however isn't a very realistic option for most freelancers however, but I'll outline the specifics to give you a fully rounded view.

Here are the realistic price ranges you'll be looking at for going down this route:

Project Deliverable:	Price Range
Offer Page Copy	$3,000 - $15,000
Email And Ad Copy	$2,500 - $7,500
Full Technical Setup	$2,500 - $10,000
Design Elements	$500 - $5,000
Ongoing Ads Management	$2,500 / month
Campaign Analysis, Optimisation & Scaling	$1,500 - $5,000 / month

That means you're going to be spending anywhere from $12,500 - $45,000 to get started, and that's just for a very basic setup.

Add that to the $30,000-50,000 for the product creation and suddenly you're looking at a total of $50,000 to $100,000 to implement a complete sales and marketing system that will generate you 5-figures a month.

As I've said, for 98% of freelancers, those figures are unrealistic.

But the problem remains that you still NEED a system like this in your business to get more clients and increase your monthly revenue, while decreasing the amount of time you spend on your business.

That's where a coaching program is the perfect middle ground. Not only do you get the same results for a small fraction of those costs, but you'll also develop the knowledge and skills to carry you forward and progress even further.

I think the main thing I want you to get out of this chapter, whether you choose to work with me and my team, or someone else, is that you *NEED* to work with someone. Going it purely alone is the fastest route to burnout and depression. **Great results are born from great teams**. You just need to get the balance that's right for you.

At the end of the day, I want you to succeed as quickly as possible. If all this book does is kickstarts a new fire in you to do just that, then awesome, I've done my job and am fulfilling my own mission in life. If you'd like me to help you further, then even better. I'm ready and waiting to get you the results you want and deserve. Just go to the link below and book in a call with us to get started:

www.growthquadrant.co/call

Just before you move onto the next chapter, I want you to answer 2 very important questions:

1. How are you going to create the products you need to grow your revenue?

2. How are you going to build your Belief Machine to find, attract and monetise your ideal clients?

Success is all about commitment. Making a decision and starting. If you move on from here with the mindset of "I'll do it later", it'll always be "later". There'll always be something "more important" to do. Another reason why it's "best left until tomorrow".

Take positive action today!

The smallest steps, when made consistently, can cover vast distances.

JAMES BRAY

REALISING YOUR POTENTIAL

WHAT TO DO NEXT?

"Smile and the world smiles with you. Give and the world gives back. Look for the good in every situation and every situation shall bless you with goodness. The world is a reflection of how we feel. Of how we perceive it. The more positive we are towards the world, the more positive the world becomes in return. We have the power to shape our world. To shape our experiences. It's all simply a matter of interpretation. Take the best of everything. Positivity is our only route to progress. To happiness."

--

And with that comes the end of this book and our time together (for the moment hopefully, anyway…)

Let's recap what we've been through:

1. In the first few chapters we looked at the major barriers to profitable growth that all freelance business owners have faced at some point in their lives. We also drilled deeper into your own business, to see where you're succeeding and where you need to refocus and tighten up. We went through some initial recommendations for improvement based on your assessment

results. From this, you should have a much clearer idea of how the **Zero Leads** process can help you.

2. Next, we looked at all the reasons why you don't want to be wasting your time with "leads" anymore. We discovered the challenges and complexities they can bring to your business, so in turn we looked at the benefits of a **Zero Leads** approach. We also balanced up this view with the problems of removing "leads" from your business.

3. In the next section of the book, we started getting into the heavier psychological stuff. We looked at a number of concepts including **The Marble Run** and how to build deep, profitable relationships with your clients using the **5 Stages Of Awareness**, the **6 Relationship Gates**, the **25 Emotional States**, the **6 Connective Qualities** and the **7 Connection Maximisers**.

4. We then swapped over to the other end of the spectrum entirely and delved into the economics, mathematics and tactics of the **Belief Machine**. We understood the concepts of the **Belief Continuum** and the **Free Client Formula** including **CPA, AOV** and **ALTV**.

5. In the following section we moved on to the practical task of defining your **Signature Offer**. Using the **Unique Framework, Irresistible Hook** and **Five Figure Drop** techniques, we mapped out the exact products and services that you need in your business for a profitable **Zero Leads** approach, completing it with the **Backwards Pricing** method. We then looked at coming up with the best product ideas using the **5 Creation Questions** and the **Level Of Knowledge** and **Level Of Implementation** question matrix.

6. And finally, in the last few chapters, we first looked at ways of optimising your **Zero Leads** system for profit using the **10 Conversion Points** and **The Conversion Triangle**. We followed this with your realistic options for setting up and implementing the **Zero Leads** method in your business. You

should now have a much clearer idea of if and where you'd need help and have a plan of action for making it happen.

You have one, and only one, next step to take…

Begin.

Whether you begin your journey with help or begin it alone, just begin.

Success won't happen overnight. It never does. Ever heard the saying "overnight success takes years"?

I'm not going to lie to you and promise you millions of dollars tomorrow. But what I *will* promise you is this, if you begin your journey today and take it one step at a time, consistently day in and day out, **you *will* find the success you're looking for.**

If you do decide you'd like us to help and support on your journey, get in touch and let's have a chat:

www.growthquadrant.co/call

We help people like you share their passion with the world, brighten the futures of others and in turn, brighten your own future in the process…

I want to thank you for giving me your time and attention in reading this book. I promised you at the beginning that I wouldn't waste it, and I really do hope that's the case. I appreciate you greatly and hope that it's got you excited about where your future could take you.

Let's make it happen!

James Bray

HOW TO GET MORE HELP

"There's a lot to learn in life. A world of infinite opportunities. Infinite lessons. Infinite paths to grow. But there are only two things we need. Two things that'll serve us well no matter the paths we choose. Kindness and gratitude. To be kind is to respect. To love. To understand and help. To have gratitude is to be thankful. Humble. Accepting of the value that others can bring to our lives. The more kindness and gratitude we have in our hearts, the more others will have in their hearts for us."

--

As part of your purchase of this book, I've also included a number of extra "bonus" resources for you. Part of the reason is to show my gratitude and appreciation for choosing to spend your time and money on what I have to say. The other part is because I really want you to succeed, so want to prepare you to begin as much as I can!

You'll find the additional free training resources within the Growth Quadrant Member's Area here:

growthquadrant.circle.so

FREE BONUS #1: The Zero Leads Tech Bible:

One of the first things to understand about the **Zero Leads** system is the actual tech that sits behind it and makes it happen. It's fine having all the theory, but if you don't know the nuts and bolts of how it all connects together, then you won't be able to launch anything. This guide lays out every app and tool you'll need to set up the **Zero Leads** system in your business.

FREE BONUS #2: The Profitable Pricing Workshop:

Pricing is vitally important, and it's usually an area that sees the most confusion (and the most mistakes). In this workshop, I'll take you through my fool-proof method for making sure you're not pricing yourself out of the market, not leaving money on the table and are able to sustain your professional and personal lives without going broke!

FREE BONUS #3: The 7-Figure Triggers Collection:

You'll have noticed that throughout this book at the start of each Chapter are short, but powerful lessons I've learned throughout my 15+ years of growing my own business and the businesses of some of the best-known brands in the world. There are 20 in this book, but there are 100 in total. This collection contains the other 80! These are the lessons of success – mainly gained through multiple failures on my part throughout my career. Heed them well!

Work With Me & My Team To Accelerate Your Results:

If this book has resonated with you and you want our help to grow into a 7-figure freelance business, please book a call with me and my team. Let's go through your ultimate goals, the challenges you're currently facing and come up with a plan together of how we can overcome those obstacles and start growing.

Remember, the key to success is *starting* that journey.

Give us a call. We can't wait to chat with you:

www.growthquadrant.co/call

ABOUT THE AUTHOR

"Your work is a gift to the world. It helps others achieve. It helps them progress. It helps them push past their problems and get closer to their goals. But it's not important. There's only one thing in this world that's important. The people you love. Friends. Family. Yourself. Don't neglect them for work's sake. Work comes second. Be there for them. They need you. And you need them. Life without work may pain your mind. But life without love will pain your soul."

--

James Bray has been at the top of sales and marketing for over 15 years. He has created and implemented multi-million-dollar strategies that have helped some of the world's largest and most recognised brands bring in more customers and grow their revenue - including The Walt Disney Company, Water Babies, SEGA and Kraft Heinz.

He has a huge passion for helping others achieve their potential and in 2019 founded **Growth Quadrant**. A coaching and consultancy business that focuses specifically on working with creative freelancers.

Outside of helping others grow their businesses, James loves to travel and see as much of the world as possible with his wife and two daughters, reading as many books as he can get his hands on and getting lost in the never-ending greatness of Apple Music playlists.

Most importantly however, James believes that relationships are the most precious thing we have, and time is the most precious thing we have to give. Being successful in business and having financial abundance is purely a way of giving us freedom and control over our time. Ultimately, we're here on this planet to help and give value to others. If we've taken care of ourselves fully, we can then fully help those in need around us. And as we do that, we leave the world in a much better place than when we came to it.

For any enquiries about podcast appearances, video shows and event speaking, please send through to support@growthquadrant.co.

Printed in Great Britain
by Amazon